The Science of Love:
Botanical Psychoanalysis

By Adeeb Kasem

"Into this house we're born,
Into this world we're thrown,
Like a dog without a bone,
An actor out alone,
Riders on the storm."
—The Doors, "Riders on the Storm"

"The end of laughter and soft lies,
The end of nights we tried to die."
—The Doors, "The End"

"The killer awoke before dawn, he put his boots on.
He took a face from the ancient gallery
And he walked on down the hall…
And he came to a door, and he looked inside.
"Father?" "Yes, son." "I want to kill you."
"Mother, I want to—"
—The Doors, "The End"

Table of Contents

<u>Preface</u>

I wrote this book due to a few perhaps naïve beliefs; among them, that writing a book can change the world and that my writings will be understood. I also wrote this book as a tribute to several philosophers whom I love: Freud, Lacan, Zizek, Wilhelm Reich, Stanislavski, Derrida, Deleuze, Guattari, Nietzsche, Marx, Althusser, La Rochefoucauld, Leopardi, Stendhal, Klossowski, Bataille, Sade, Sacher-Masoch, Proust, and Jim Morrison. Books should only ever be written out of love. I love a few dozen other philosophers as well, but contemplating the works of these particular philosophers occasioned the thoughts that I have recorded in this book. I believe in a new rationalism. I believe that Reason is the means by which we can solve all of the problems which plague us.

To begin to understand the concepts of psychoanalysis, particularly the Oedipus complex and primal repression, let us perform a dramaturgy of early childhood. Let us apply Stanislavski's *magic if* to childhood, and let us ask, "If I were an infant, what would I experience in my daily life?" Inevitably, we would experience our mother and our father, who are an inescapable and large presence in the early years of our lives. We may also ask, "If I were an infant, what would I want? What would I want from my mother? What would I want from my father?" Thus, we can begin to understand that the drama of childhood is the drama of the Oedipus complex. In psychology, origins matter, because insofar as the Oedipus complex is still alive within our unconscious, the past is alive within us, and the Oedipus complex, our psychical origin, continues to produce effects upon us.

A fantasy is the object of a motivation. Because the concept of fantasy has operational value for actors (in the form of the concept of motivation), who reverse-engineer and reproduce the psyche and behaviour, it also has operational value in therapy, which consists, or at least ought to consist, of understanding the motivations of the analysand, especially those motivations which produce morbid symptoms, in order to, ideally, modify or eliminate the patient's pathological motivations and thereby cure the patient of his illness.

We do not escape the influence of the family merely by denying its influence. Rather, we can only free ourselves of the family by rooting it out of our unconscious, from where it exerts its invisible influence upon us. Freud's theory of the Oedipus complex and its repression gives us the means by which to free ourselves of the family. It is only by acknowledging the deep ways in which our parents wounded us that we can even begin to heal those wounds, and thereby become healthier, fuller, more realistic, more rational, and lighter human beings. Or, if we prefer the Nietzschean formulation: humankind is defined by neurosis, and to overcome humanity, to become something more than human, to become the overman (or overwoman), we must first cure ourselves of our humanity by curing ourselves of our neurosis.

The Dramaturgy of Desiring-Machines

Deleuze and Guattari write, "Desiring-machines are binary machines, obeying a law or set of rules governing associations: one machine is always coupled with another. The productive synthesis, the production of production, is inherently connective in nature: "and…" "and then…" This is because there is always a flow-producing machine, and another machine connected to it that interrupts or draws off part of this flow (the breast—the mouth). And because the first machine is in turn connected to another whose flow it interrupts or partially drains off, the binary series is linear in every direction" (1972/1977, p. 5). Deleuze and Guattari define a machine as a "system of interruptions," i.e. a system of flows and interruptions of flows (1972/1977, p. 36). A desiring-machine is a system of flows of libido and interruptions of flows of libido. A desiring-machine is an organismic unit and a motivational unit (or a "unit objective," a unit aim, to borrow Stanislavski's term), a unit of motivation and a unit of sexual desire with organismic qualities which comprises part of an organism. A desiring-machine is an erotogenic system which strives to possess an object of desire, which is the fantasy it strives to fulfil, or the objective it strives to achieve. The object of desire is fantasy, and fantasy is the object of desire. There are two fundamental kinds of desiring-machines: flow-ingesting machines and flow-producing machines. The former is analogous to the oral erotogenic zone and the latter is analogous to the anal erotogenic zone.

Concerning the oral zone, Freud writes, "Here sexual activity has not yet been separated from the ingestion of food; nor are opposite currents within the activity differentiated. The *object* of both activities is the same; the sexual *aim* consists in the incorporation of the object..." (1962, p. 64). The erotogenic organ-machine of the mouth strives to possess the material flow of milk which is simultaneously and primarily the flow of libido, or psychosemiotic flow, constitutive of its object of desire. The mouth strives to ingest, or introject, i.e. appropriate and consume, this psychosemiotic flow, and thereby to possess its object of desire. Analogously, the flow-ingesting machine strives to possess its object of desire by ingesting, or introjecting, a particular psychosemiotic flow (which is also a material flow, or rather, which also has a material correlate). The flow-producing machine, on the other hand, has as its object of desire the retention or expulsion of a psychosemiotic flow (which is also a material flow). Both flow-ingesting machines and flow-producing machines are driven by the pleasure principle, the striving for the total reduction of excitations, or unpleasure, and in this quality both their objects of desire, despite the difference in the direction of psychosemiotic fluid, are the same, because the aim of both is the total reduction of excitations (this aim, however, is never truly achieved, a point which we shall return to later). The flow-ingesting machine strives to reduce excitations by ingesting its object of desire, whereas the flow-producing machine strives to reduce excitations by some combination of the retention and/or expulsion of its psychosemiotic flow.

However, the function of a desiring-machine is more complex than a binary identity allows us to describe, since a desiring-machine may function as both a flow-ingesting machine and a flow-producing machine, either at different times or at the same time depending on the machine in question and the circumstance. A desiring-machine is binary only in terms of the value of the direction of psychosemiotic flows: either inward or outward. But the function of a desiring-machine and its connections with other desiring-machines are multi-valued, meaning that desiring-machines are more accurately described as multiplicity machines, rather than binary machines. The law governing the coupling of machines is the law of multiplicity. For example, the mouth, considered as an erotogenic zone, performs a variety of functions even in infancy: sucking, breathing, spitting, crying, laughing, burping, and vomiting, each of which is an activity, in metapsychological terms, concerning flows of libido, or psychosemiotic flows, and driven by the pleasure principle. The oral zone, or labial zone, because it functions as both a flow-ingesting machine and a flow-producing machine in a variety of ways and is connected to a variety of other desiring-machines, is more accurately described as an *erotogenic system* rather than an erotogenic zone, since it is not a simple topography but a complex combination of forces whose function is determined by its use and whose possible uses are various. Even considering merely the relationship of the mouth and the breast between the infant and the mother, the relationship is one of multiplicity and reciprocal flows of libido in which each desiring-machine serves both as flow-ingesting machine and flow-producing machine simultaneously. The mouth is a flow-ingesting machine which siphons off flows of milk and libido from the flow-producing breast, and the mouth is a flow-producing machine which expulses flows of tactile stimulation and libido which the flow-ingesting machine of the breast, which is also an erotogenic system, receives and ingests. The anal zone, too, is a multiplicity machine: it is not only a flow-producing machine which expulses flows of faecal matter, but it is also, on the other hand, a flow-ingesting machine which ingests flows of faecal matter from the digestive system, in addition to being a flow-ingesting machine that receives and ingests tactile stimulation (viz. when it expulses faecal matter). Each of our organs, including our sensory organs, is primarily a metapsychological apparatus, i.e. a desiring-machine.

Thus we must amend our earlier definition of desiring-machines simply in terms of "units" (organismic unit, motivational unit, erotogenic unit, and unit objective), since a desiring-machine is not merely a bivalent, passive vessel for flows of libido, but is a multi-valent, active computational module for flows of libido. A desiring-machine is indeed a unit, but more specifically it is a *unit-structure* or *unit-system*, both a unit of a larger whole and a system unto itself, a combination of forces which function together within the larger, overarching combination of forces that is an organism. A desiring-machine is a unit-system of motivation, a unit-system objective, a unit-system of sexual desire. Moreover, in consideration of the multi-valent and complex operations performed by desiring-machines, it is evident that a desiring-machine is an intelligent system, that is to say, a desiring-machine's functioning evinces that it is capable of sensory integration, associative memory, decision-making, and the control of behaviour. An organism consists of desiring-machines, and desiring-machines are proto-organisms constitutive of an organism. We shall return to the topic of the intelligence of desiring-machines later.

A desiring-machine is a unit-system of desiring-production. We agree with Deleuze and Guattari that all organic processes are processes of libidinal production (cf. 1972/1977, p. 4), but we disagree that even inorganic forces can be described in terms of libidinal production. Although metaphysically it is inescapable that even the inorganic world consists of animate forces, and not inanimate matter, it is just as pragmatically meaningless to develop a metapsychology of inorganic forces, since reducing the inorganic world to mere objects is indubitably useful in the physical sciences. However, we argue that Nietzsche's pan-psychism, which considers both the organic and inorganic world as consisting of psychic forces, is indispensable for psychology, sociology, anthropology, and the humanities, and that it is the only rational solution to the mind-body problem (cf. *The Science of Self-Actualization*, Kasem 2018, pp. 98-140). We agree with biosemioticians that life and semiotics are fundamentally equivalent to each other, and it is in consideration of the semiotic property of organic processes in combination with the psychoanalytic finding that life is equivalent to the libido and that life consists of economic systems of libido, that we reach the conclusion that all organic processes are processes of production. But what is production? And what is its relation to semiotics, which is the science of interpretation, and really the science of writing? To begin with, it is evident that writing and production are fundamentally equivalent, whether one considers writing the production of signs or production a form of writing. Pragmatically and in terms of effectivity, the fundamental question is that of production.

Deleuze and Guattari argue that the conceptual distinction between production, distribution, and consumption only arises in particular circumstances, namely those of capitalism, since it "presupposes (as Marx has demonstrated) not only the existence of capital and the division of labor, but also the false consciousness that the capitalist being acquires, both of itself and of the supposedly fixed elements within an overall process" (1972/1977, p. 4). The defining elements of capitalism, including the existence of capital, the division of labour into the labourer and the owner of the means of production, and the false consciousness of the capitalist being which falsifies all the elements, relations, and processes of production, gives rise to the separation of production, distribution, and consumption into relatively independent circuits. However, in other economic systems, namely those which precede capitalism, where one or more of the defining elements of capitalism are absent, the capitalist distinction of production, distribution, and consumption into relatively independent circuits is also absent. Of course, the fundamental productive processes of life all precede the capitalist socioeconomic system, and since the elements of capitalism are largely absent from fundamental organic processes, the distinction of production, distribution and consumption into relatively independent circuits is likewise absent from fundamental organic processes. The fundamental organic processes are those which comprise the psychic economy of living organisms. This means that even in capitalist socioeconomic systems, the fundamental and defining processes of production at work function quite differently from the superficial production process of capitalism, with its false distinctions and false consciousness, since the basis of all socioeconomic systems, including capitalism, is the psychic economy of living organisms. The glaring, sober truth that resides in reason is that there is no such thing as relatively independent circuits of an economic system.

Deleuze and Guattari write that in the biological economy of the psyche, i.e. in the psychic economy of the organism, "production is immediately consumption and a recording process (*enregistrement*), without any sort of mediation, and the recording process and consumption directly determine production, though they do so within the production process itself. Hence everything is production: *production of productions*, of actions and of passions; *productions of recording processes*, of distributions and of co-ordinates that serve as points of reference; *productions of consumptions*, of sensual pleasures, of anxieties, and of pain. Everything is production, since the recording processes are immediately consumed, immediately consummated, and these consumptions directly reproduced. This is the first meaning of the process as we use the term: incorporating recording and consumption within production itself, thus making them productions of one and the same process" (1972/1977, p. 4). Production, distribution (recording), and consumption are in fact the same process, that of production. The production of productions is the production of actions and passions, that is to say, the production of motivations or drives, the passions which directly yield actions. The production of productions is not only the generation of motivations, nor only the production process that result directly from motivations, but it is also the very process of motivation itself, for motivation itself is a process of production. We recognize that desire, motivation, and production are fundamentally equivalent to each other. Desiring-production may also be called motivation-production. The production of recording processes is the production of co-ordinates that serve as points of reference, that is to say, it is the production of memories, or the encoding of memories. The production of consumptions is the production of sensual pleasures, anxieties, and pains, that is to say, it is the production of emotions, if we mean here the strictly Stanislavskian concept of emotion, the psychological state that results directly from the motivation in relation to the scenario of conflict in which the motivation occurs. However, we also recognize the truth of the Nietzschean concept of emotion, which is that emotions are equivalent to the drives and that they are immanent and originary. Nietzsche and Stanislavski describe two different types of emotion, both of which exist. For the sake of clarity, we shall refer to Stanislavski's concept of emotion as "emotion" and Nietzsche's concept of emotion as "affect." We may say that emotions and affects are both types of feeling, and that feeling is immanent and originary. Feeling, as in "What does it feel like to be…?" Affects are the feelings which *are* drives, and emotions are the feelings which result from motivations. Affects produce emotions. Motivation is immediately the production of emotions and the encoding of memories, without any sort of mediation, and the encoding of memories and the production of emotions directly determine motivation, though they do so within the process of motivation itself. Everything is motivation, since the encoding of memories is immediately the production of emotions, and these emotions are directly reproduced. Motivation incorporates within itself both the encoding of memories and the production of emotions, thus making motivation, memory, and emotion productions of one and the same production process, that of desiring-production.

Derrida (1997) argues that writing, a system of difference and mediation, is originary and immanent. Everything is writing because everything is a system of difference and mediation (Derrida, 1997). Therefore, acting is a form of writing. But writing, since it is the product of a motivation, is a form of acting. It is clear that writing and acting are at bottom fundamentally equivalent to each other. Desiring-production is the structure of writing, especially when writing is considered from the perspective of the writer, or rather, the writing-machine; that is to say, desiring-production is what it feels like to write from the inside of the writing process. The language of desiring-production and the currency of the economy of desiring-production are quantities of libido, which are quantities of excitations. Motivations, memories, and emotions are all quantities of libido and quantities of excitations, which is part of what makes possible the functional unity of these processes within the process of desiring-production. Nietzsche's theory of memory, which we have elsewhere described alternatively as the mnemonics of cruelty, the theory of impression, mnemonic inscription, and mnemic inscription, is that pain inscribes memories, or to phrase it another way, the higher the quantity of excitation, the greater the memorability of a sign (cf. Kasem 2018, pp. 202-203). Deleuze and Guattari's theory of desiring-production, especially considering the modifications we have made to it, help explain Nietzsche's theory of the mnemonics of cruelty. The production of recording is the mnemonics of cruelty, or mnemonic inscription, and it is an essential component of the functioning of motivation itself. Motivation is a quantity of excitations the content of which is the lust to possess the object of desire; because the object of desire is always merely a fantasy, possessing it is effectively impossible, and the failure to possess the object of desire is inevitable and systemic, an essential component in the very functioning of desire itself; the failure to possess the object of desire results in a recycling of some quantity of excitations back into the motivation, and this recycled quantity of excitations, which have as their content the movement-images constitutive of the failure to possess the object of desire, is both the production of recordings, which is the encoding of memories, and the surplus value of excitations which is immediately consumed-consummated, which is the emotions. These emotions and memories, in turn, fuel the motivation and its quest to possess the object of desire, which it will inevitably fail.

Raw Drive and Primary Lack

The body without organs, which constitutes the organism as such, consists of libido, fantasies, movement-images, and raw drives. Bataille discovered within Nietzsche's texts and within himself a drive devoid of any possible object: "I'm on fire with painful longings, persisting in me like unsatisfied desire…Whatever great or necessary actions come to mind, none answers to this feverishness. I'm speaking of moral concerns—of discovering some object that surpasses all others in value!...Compared to the moral ends normally advanced, the object I refer to is incommensurable. Moral ends seem deceptive and lustreless. Still, only moral ends translate to acts (aren't they determined as a demand for definite acts?)" (1945/1992, p. xvii). Raw drive is this perpetually and systemically unsatisfied desire, this painful and impossible longing. Actions are driven by motivations to possess particular objects of desire. Moral ends are objects of desire, and objects of desire are moral ends. Raw drive does not translate to a specific act because it lacks a specific object of desire. Raw drive is impossible longing, a longing for the impossible, because no possible object of desire is commensurate with its need. Because raw drive is devoid of any possible object of desire, it is also devoid of the possibility of pleasure or happiness, because it can never experience the satisfaction that would result from possessing an object of desire. Therefore, raw drive is in essence pure pain, since it is a quantity of excitations, even an excess of excitations, which, because it is devoid of the possibility of attaining pleasure, is necessarily a state of unpleasure, i.e. a state of pain. Raw drive exists and persists as the painful longing of unsatisfied and insatiable desire. Raw drive is raw passion, pure pain and pure passion. A quantity of raw drive is a quantity of pain.

Raw drive is objectless desire, desire without an object and without content: pure will, the pure force of motivation without an object. Raw drive is raw energy. Raw drive is, to borrow a phrase from Iggy Pop and The Stooges, *raw power*. Desire, at bottom, is desire without any object, a purely subjective force and the force of pure subjectivity. Raw power is the will to power in its primary and primordial state: pure will and pure power, the pure lust for possession without any possible object which it can possess. Raw drive is raw violence, pure libido and pure violence. Raw drive is the drive of drives. Raw drive is the fluid of the psyche. Every motivation, every drive, is constituted by and animated by raw drive.

Objectless desire drives desire for an object, which is why desire can never be satisfied. Raw drive is rhizomatic. The drives do not operate in the manner of a tree, beginning with raw drive and then branching out to diverse motivations with specific objects, because raw drive is immanent, it exists and operates within every drive with a specific object as its basis, its engine, and its fuel. Raw drive is a multiplicity, it is polyvocal and it has no inherent unity because it is a system of difference and mediation. Raw drive has a special affinity with music, because music is perhaps the best metaphor for raw drive and because music is an example of raw drive. Like music, raw drive consists of objectless and contentless affects, or objectless and contentless passions; pure affects, pure passions. The qualitatively different kinds of raw drives, being as they are devoid of content, are best described as different flavours, colours, timbres, or tones. Raw drives may also be described as raw images, raw movement-images, pure images, or pure movement-images; they are images without content, of which the models are music and multi-coloured stroboscopic lamps, the free play of pure sounds and pure colours. Raw drives are raw impulses, or pure impulses.

La Rochefoucauld (2007, I: I, pp.147-151) writes that all living beings are motivated by self-love. We ask, which self? Depending on which self, the nature of the self-love necessarily differs. That is to say, considering the self as the dominant drive of an organism, and considering that there are diverse drives (e.g. greed, vanity, generosity, independence), the conditions that would satisfy any one drive, however temporarily, necessarily differ from the conditions that would satisfy any other drive. La Rochefoucauld's theory of self-love bears a strong affinity with Freud's theory that the drives are in essence narcissistic; the essential narcissism of the drives means that a drive functions primarily to satisfy itself. All drives are selfish. Each drive has its own form of self-love. Raw drive, too, being a drive, has an urge to satisfy itself, a form of self-love. But having no object, what are the conditions that would satisfy it? The defining quality of raw drive is that it has no object, and it is this very absence of an object, this lack, that is the defining condition of its existence. The self-love of raw drive is its love for the condition of existence of its self, lack. The "object" of raw drive, or raw desire, is its very objectlessness, the void or primary lack that defines and drives it. This state of primary lack, if it had any real existence independent of being the phantasm of raw drives, would resemble the Epicurean concept of death, that is to say, a state of absolute nothingness, devoid of any possible sensation, thought, or feeling.

As Nietzsche argues in his later work, and as we recount in *The Science of Self-Actualization* (Kasem 2018, pp. 98-140), there is no inanimate matter, but only animate and living psychic forces. Even the inorganic world consists of psychic forces, that is to say, of libido and excitations. If the drives were truly conservative and really had as their aim the repetition of an earlier state of things, then they would desire the increase of their quantity of excitations to the horrible intensity of inorganic forces, for no other purpose than to mimic their senseless pure discharge of energy, and they would do so repeatedly; in other words, the drives would not seek the state of death as their aim. However, the drives, insofar as they seek pleasure, meaning that they seek the cessation of excitations, also seek the state of death, for the state of death is precisely the cessation of excitations. The economy of the pleasure principle is equivalent to the economy of the death drive, since both have as their motive the absolute reduction of excitations. Thus, fantasy is not the wish to return to a past state, but the wish to arrive at a future state; a future state which is, unbeknownst to the subject, purely imaginary and invariably unattainable.

The drive to life and the drive to death are not opposed to each other, but are one and the same drive, the sex drive, i.e. the libido. For if we question the notion of life, we may ask, "Which life?", that is to say, "Which drive?", and thereby discover that the different forms of desire, each with their own particular object of desire, are each their own form of life, and these objects of desire are each a form of death, since the pleasure that they represent means the total reduction of excitations and therefore also means death, or nothingness. The drives of life reproduce themselves only to reproduce the wish for death that is their aim, therefore the life-drives and the death drives are in actuality one and the same drive, which we may call the libido or the sex-drive (Q.E.D.). Eros and Thanatos are one and the same.

D.H. Lawrence writes on love: "We have pushed a process into a goal. The aim of any process is not the perpetuation of that process, but the completion thereof…The process should work to a completion, not to some horror of intensification and extremity wherein the soul and the body ultimately perish" (1976, pp. 200-201; as quoted in Deleuze and Guattari 1972/1977, p. 5). Lawrence here criticizes the ethical doctrine that desire ought to have as its aim the increase of its quantity of intensity, which would mean an exponential increase whose sheer intensity would destroy the balance that maintains organic processes and so would result in the destruction of the organism. Lawrence argues that the aim of the process of desire ought to be the completion of the process, which would mean the absolute reduction of a desire's quantity of intensity (the quantity of excitation = the quantity of intensity). However, the aim and function of desire are natural, biological, and unconscious processes, and cannot be determined by ethical doctrines, for they are never mere matters of conscious will. In this passage, Lawrence inadvertently expresses both the natural, biological aim of desire, "completion," and its actual, biological, and non-teleological functioning, which is incompletion and perpetuation. In nature, the sex drive and the death drive are fused, they are one and the same drive. Desire is always desire for the total cessation of excitations, never a desire for the increase of excitations in itself. If desire is ever a desire for the increase of excitations, it is only ever as a means to an end, the end being the cessation of excitations (e.g. the libidinal economy of masochism). It is precisely because the cessation of excitations is impossible that the drives sustain themselves, both fuelled by the excitations they inevitably acquire and driven onto further activity by the impossible goal of eliminating all excitations. The drives desire the completion of the process of desire, but because this completion is impossible and unattainable, their activity, which aims at the completion of the process, results in the perpetuation of the process, which means in some cases "the horror of intensification and extremity."

Nietzsche's logic of the will to power, taken to its furthest extreme, as we have taken it here, leads to self-criticism and to the inescapable conclusion that the will to power is in fact the "will to nothingness" which Nietzsche so dreaded, disavowed, and opposed to his concept of the will to power. The will to power is the lust for possession, but this lust, insofar as it is perpetually and systemically unsatisfied, meaning that it is perpetually and systemically unsatisfied with itself as it seeks its own gratification, seeks as its object of desire something outside of itself and other than itself, even something which is the opposite of itself; because the will to power is always a positive quantity of excitations, its opposite would be the total absence of excitations, that is to say a quantity of zero excitations, which is, in other words, the state of nothingness, meaning that the will to power is in fact the will to nothingness. In biological terms, the will to power is the sex drive, or the libido; here we are in agreement with the scientific discoveries of Freud.

Because the will to power is a biological energy, we must identify it according to its biological reality, and an examination of the psyche reveals that all forms of psychic energy are forms of the libido. We accept Freud's conclusion that the libido is governed by the pleasure principle, the desire for the cessation of excitations; our amendment to Freud's theory here is our identification of the equivalence of the pleasure principle of the libido with the death drive, outlined above. This means that many of Nietzsche's conclusions, especially those in his book *On the Genealogy of Morals*, need to be radically revised. However, that being said, many of his conclusions on the nature of the drives and on pleasure remain pertinent to drive psychology, and we have built upon them here.

According to Klossowski, a *phantasm*, or fantasy, is an anticipated excitation (1997, p. 47). However, as we have rigorously demonstrated, a phantasm, or fantasy, is actually an anticipated total cessation of excitations. The originary fantasy, raw fantasy, or proto-fantasy, is that of primary lack. Each fantasy is a form of lack, meaning ultimately that it is a form of primary lack. In his book *Love*, Stendhal frequently repeats the formula, "Beauty is the promise of pleasure," which he alternatively phrases as "Beauty is a potentiality for pleasure." He means that beauty is the anticipation of, or the potentiality for, the cessation of pain, which is evident since he consistently describes desire as a state of tension, even of agony. Potentialities for pleasure are pure potentialities, potentialities which can never be actualized. Beauty is fantasy, fantasy is beauty. In his novel *This Side of Paradise*, F. Scott Fitzgerald writes, "Beauty is agony and the end of agony." As the object of desire, beauty means the cessation of excitations; however, because the pursuit of the object of desire is invariably a failure, the object of desire yields only the accumulation of excitations, that is to say, the accumulation of pain. Proust, in his novel *In Search of Lost Time*, writes, "In love there is permanent suffering." Although the object of desire is always the potentiality for a state of zero intensity, the actual effect of the object of desire upon the drive is always the perpetuation and accumulation of quantities of intensity, hence why the drives are perpetually in a state of dissatisfaction, i.e. desire is always a state of permanent suffering.

Leopardi writes that pleasure is never experienced, that it is a matter of pure speculation; it is never a reality and always a fantasy, "a feeling that man conceives by thinking, but does not experience; or, to put it better, a concept and not a feeling" (2017, p. 62). Pleasure is an abstraction, a fabrication by a drive, the nature of the pleasure differing according to the nature of the drive which fabricates the concept of it. Leopardi continues, writing that even during an allegedly pleasurable time, the drives are never content, never satisfied, even if the energy expended to acquire that moment was prodigious; Leopardi writes, "you are always waiting for some greater and truer enjoyment, in which such pleasure really consists; and you go on constantly looking forward to future moments of that same pleasure" (ibid). The drives sustain their own activity, which is the very activity of living, only by fabricating concepts of pleasure, or fantasies, which they then strive to attain, maintaining their life by virtue of the fact that what they seek to attain, which means ultimately the state of zero intensity, is impossible to attain. Leopardi writes that allegedly enjoyable activity always comes to an end before it can bring true satisfaction to the subject, thereby leaving the subject with two illusions: that the subject will experience a greater and truer pleasure in a future moment, and that the subject has experienced pleasure in a past moment (the moment in question of alleged pleasure, which has inevitably become a past moment) (ibid, pp. 62-63). For example, one does not bite a fruit simply once, but keeps biting into it in the hopes of finding a pleasure that will satiate one's drive, and one does this until one is no longer able to, either because the fruit has been depleted or because one has no more room in one's stomach; one does not stop because one is truly satisfied, and if true satisfaction were ever attained, it would leave one with no impetus to do anything; yet one hopes that in the future one will attain a greater and truer pleasure by repeating the same activity, and one believes that one has indeed experienced pleasure through the activity; the same is true of sexual activity, and indeed more generally of time spent with objects of one's affection. In addition, the belief that one has experienced pleasure in a past moment is a present fantasy, meaning that nostalgia is actually an orientation towards the future, since it is the anticipation of a future pleasure, namely by means of repeating the past actions which one believes has brought one pleasure.

The relation between raw drive and primary lack (proto-fantasy, or simply, fantasy), is one of positive feedback. On the one hand, it is evident that raw drive is driven by fantasy, that fantasy is the aim of raw drive, that raw drive strives for the possession of primary lack, meaning that fantasy must precede raw drive and that fantasy produces raw drive. On the other hand, the fantasy of primary lack represents nothingness and non-being, that is to say, it cannot have any substantial and real existence and it is merely a representation and a concept. Thus, raw drive must precede fantasy, since a fantasy is a concept fabricated by a drive. In other words, fantasy is a product of raw drive, raw drive produces fantasy. Moreover, in its repeated and inevitable failures to possess pleasure, raw drive accumulates more quantities of raw drive and thus produces more fantasy. Hence the positive feedback cycle of raw drive and fantasy: raw drive produces fantasy and fantasy drives raw drive, raw drive accumulates higher quantities of raw drive and raw drive produces more fantasy. Raw drive is a pure fluid in a free state, flowing without interruption, constituting the body without organs; but because raw drive is inseparable from and coextensive with fantasy, or primary lack, this also means that fantasy is a pure fluid in a free state, flowing without interruption and constituting the body without organs.

The origin of this positive feedback cycle between raw drive and fantasy is a historical question, it is the question of the very origin of life, for raw drive and fantasy are inseparable from each other and their relation is the defining relation of life. Motivation, fantasy, memory, and consciousness are all elements of desiring-production, and to ask of their origin is to ask of the origin of desiring-production, the origin of economy itself. The question of the origin of desiring-production, which is the structure of all desire, including raw drive, likewise, is also the question of the origin of life. The question of the origin of life is a question not only for biochemistry, but also, and perhaps even primarily, a question for metapsychology and biosemiotics. The psychoanalytic theory of the origin of life is beyond the scope of the present work, but deserves further inquiry.

The Production of Fantasy

Klossowski writes, "Nothing exists apart from *impulses* that are essentially *generative* of *phantasms*" (1997, p. 133). Nothing exists apart from drives that are essentially productive of fantasies. The production of fantasies is an essential and defining function of drives. The drives are essentially productive of fantasies, that is to say, of potentialities for the absolute reduction of excitations, and they are condemned to this productivity because the absolute reduction of excitations is impossible and unattainable. We have seen above how fantasy is lack, and how desire necessarily implies lack; we are in agreement with much of the work of Lacan, who also discovered that fantasy is lack and that desire at bottom means lack, although the nuances of our theory of fantasy and lack differ greatly from Lacan's. We accept Deleuze and Guattari's conclusion that desire is a positive and productive force, but we find their account of desire and fantasy insufficient, and we find their rejection of the concepts fantasy and lack to be untenable. Both desiring-production and lack exist, and both are primary, as paradoxical as that may seem at first glance. The positivity of desire and the negativity of lack, the productivity of desire and the anti-productivity of lack, coexist in a positive feedback cycle that is inherent to the functioning of desire. Desire, in addition to being characterized as positive production, the positive existence of a force that is productive, may also be characterized as negative production, since it is the production of negative entities (the non-being of lack). Lack, in addition to being characterized as negative, since it is what is missing, may also be characterized as positive, since it is the positive presence of nothingness, the positive presence of a negative substance, and because it is what drives desire (it is the quasi-cause of desire); nothingness (i.e. lack) is a negative force with positive existence. Desiring-production is indeed a process of production, but only because desiring-production is the production of fantasies, that is to say, the production of lack. We draw our conclusions on desiring-production, distinct from Deleuze and Guattari's conclusions, from the Dionysian drama of desire, that is to say, from the critical analysis and dramaturgy of the subjectivity of desire, especially in relation to its conflicts with the Real, most prominently embodied in the form of the other, and we build upon the findings of Leopardi, Stendhal, Proust, and Stanislavski, as well as of Freud, Lacan and Nietzsche.

In his novel *In Search of Lost Time*, Proust repeatedly returns to the conclusion that desire is a purely subjective phenomenon, and he illustrates this conclusion in myriad ways, but most often through the distinction he makes between what we term the *object of desire* and the *other of desire*. The object of desire is a fantasy which exists only in the mind of the subject, and here we mean desire for another person (as opposed to object fetishism), which invariably is based on a fantasy of who the other person is, and not who the other person is in reality; whereas the other of desire is the reality of the other, it is the subjectivity of the other independent of the self and the intersubjective relation between the self and the other. The object of desire exists purely in the mind of the subject, which means that it differs from and is wholly absent from the real existence of the other of desire. Lacan describes the Real as the impossible and what does not work; the other of desire, who is the Real embodied, is the impossible, meaning the absence of the object of desire, that which makes the satisfaction of the subject's desire impossible, and the other of desire is what does not work, that is to say, that which differs from the object of desire and so does not satisfy the subject's desire.

The object of desire, or beauty, is purely imaginary, it is a product of the imagination, a conclusion which Stendhal often reiterates in his book *Love*. In *Love*, Stendhal describes the primary activity of desire, the production of beauties, potentialities for pleasure, or fantasies, as *crystallization*. Stendhal calls the production of fantasies crystallization because the process resembles what happens to a leafless bough when it is thrown into the salt mines of Salzburg and pulled out after several months: it is studded with scintillating crystals (1957, p. 45). Crystallization is the production of potentialities for pleasure, that is to say, potentialities for the total reduction of excitations. The drives are essentially generative of fantasies, and crystallization is this process of the generation of fantasies. As Stendhal writes, each drive has its own mode of crystallization, each drive produces different fantasies according to its own nature (1957, p. 52). But crystallization is the same in all drives in that it is the production of objects of desire, that is to say, the production of impossible and unattainable fantasies. The forces that the subject appropriates and consumes from the environment, even those which the subject appropriates from the other of desire, are never commensurate or equivalent to the object of desire, nor can they ever be, since the object of desire is a pure fantasy with no real existence in the world external to and independent of the subject.

Leopardi writes, "Therefore whoever consents to live does so really, to no other effect, and for no other purpose, than to dream; that is, to believe that there is enjoyment to come, or that he has had some enjoyment. Both ideas are false and imaginary" (2017, p. 63). A drive is a will to have power over its object of desire, but its object of desire is actually wholly imaginary, a fabrication and an imagining by that very drive. The object of desire is a *fantasy* and a *dream-work* in the strictly Freudian sense of *wish-fulfilment*. Crystallization is dreaming, dreaming is crystallization. We dream when we are awake because our drives are forever fabricating objects of desire, objects of desire which we are destined to search for but never to find, since they have no real existence and are nothing more than phantoms of our imagination.

A drive is a unit-system of desiring-production. Desire is a process of production, it produces objects of desire. However, the process of production is more robust than the mere fact of production because in order for production to occur, the conditions of production must exist and these conditions must be actively made to exist, i.e. they must be reproduced. Marx writes that the mode of production is the infrastructure, or base, of a socioeconomic system, while the superstructure consists of the ideological apparatus, which reproduces the conditions of existence of the mode of production. We accept Marx's structuralist concept of the socioeconomic system due to the logic of production, which requires the conditions of production to be reproduced in order for production to occur; however, we argue Marx's concept applies primarily and uniquely to the psyche and its psychic economy, which is a socioeconomic system constituted by the multiplicity of subjectivities of psychic forces. (cf. Althusser 2001; Kasem 2018, pp.161-295).

Fantasy is the mode of production of a drive. To be more specific, the mode of crystallization is the mode of production of a drive. Each type of drive has its own distinct mode of crystallization, i.e. it has its own distinct type of fantasy, and thus it has its own distinct mode of production. Each form of life is a mode of fantasizing, and has no reason for being other than fantasizing. The psyche is governed by the pleasure principle because fantasy is the infrastructure, the very heart and engine, of the psyche; the pleasure principle may also be called the fantasy principle. The products of crystallization, the crystals of crystallization, may also be called fantasy-crystals, pleasure-crystals, fantasy-products, or fantasy-derivations; they are not only derivations of primary lack, but are also derivations of the primal fantasy, which in human beings means a variation of either the Oedipus complex or the Electra complex. Althusser, recounting Marx's concepts of the infrastructure and superstructure, writes that the superstructure, although it has a relative autonomy, is "determined in the last instance" by the infrastructure (2001, pp. 90-91). The ideological apparatus is a module of the mode of production, a module which specializes in reproducing the conditions of production. We have demonstrated above that pleasure and fantasy are equivalent to each other, and that pleasure is in fact a mere idea, or concept. The fact that fantasy-crystals are mere ideas does indeed blur the distinction between the mode of production and the ideological apparatus, since both systems produce ideas. Moreover, in order to reproduce the conditions of production of the primary idea of fantasy, the ideological apparatus must include traces of fantasy in much of the ideology, or ideas, that it produces. However, the distinction between the infrastructure and the superstructure nonetheless holds, since the fantasy is the primary idea or dominant idea produced, and the ideas produced by the ideological apparatus only serve the function of reproducing the conditions of production of the dominant idea. Furthermore, a unit-system of desiring-production is not only a system for the production of ideas, but also a system for the production of actions, a system of practices.

In addition to producing ideas, the ideological apparatus also produces "material conditions." The conditions of existence of a drive's mode of production are the conditions which allow the production of the fantasy that defines and determines that drive. Much of what we call "material conditions" are in fact modules of the ideological apparatus of the psyche, for they reproduce the psyche's mode of production, which is unconscious. A "material" mode of production, for example industrial capitalism, is in fact a module of the superstructure of the psychic economy, since its primary function is to reproduce the conditions of the mode of production of the psyche, which is "immaterial," and which in this example means the fantasy of capital, which means, in plain language, the idea that money will bring one happiness, or in even plainer language, greed.

Raw drive, too, has a structure of infrastructure and superstructure. The mode of production of raw drive is primary lack.

The higher the quantity of raw drive, the higher the quantity of lack produced, and consequently the greater the feeling of lack, i.e. the feeling of need. The conditions of production of raw drive are the conditions which allow the production of primary lack. Desire is always the desire for a fantasy, and because a fantasy is always a *potentiality* for pleasure, i.e. a purely imaginary *future* event in which the state of zero intensity is experienced, desire is always "progressive" and never "conservative." Desire has "a need to restore an earlier state of things" only if this earlier state of things are part of the conditions for the production of a fantasy, a fantasy which invariably refers to a purely imaginary future.

Each desiring-machine appropriates and consumes flows of excitations. We agree with Nietzsche when he writes that "pleasure" and "pain" are intellectual judgements, intellectual processes "in which a judgement makes itself unmistakeably heard" (WLN, N14, 173). However, we agree only because we consider these "intellectual judgements" to be judgements made by the unconscious, or more specifically, by the ideological apparatus of the unconscious. "Pleasure," or more accurately, *quasi-pleasure*, and "pain" are interpretations of excitations by the unconscious. That is to say, they are ideological constructs produced by the ideological apparatus of the unconscious. In everyday language, people say they experience "pleasure," however, as we have demonstrated above, citing the findings of Leopardi, true pleasure is never experienced, and memories of pleasures in past moments are retrospective fantasy-constructs; to those sensations which approach pleasure, without ever arriving at it, we give the name *quasi-pleasure*. The false consciousness of the subject of desire describes certain activities as "pleasures" which are in reality merely "quasi-pleasures." The ideological apparatus of a drive interprets an excitation as quasi-pleasure if that excitation reproduces the conditions of production of that drive, and a drive interprets an excitation as pain if that excitation is antithetical to the conditions of production of that drive. Nietzsche writes that pleasure is a form of pain (WLN, N40, 42). This is true if by "pleasure" we mean "quasi-pleasure," since both quasi-pleasure and pain are quantities of excitations, which, as we have demonstrated above, means dissatisfaction and pain, since a quantity of excitation is a quantity of drive and a drive is perpetually and essentially a state of dissatisfaction and pain. However, we reject much else of Nietzsche's theory of pleasure, even as it regards quasi-pleasure; a quasi-pleasure does not consist merely in a high quantity of excitations, nor in the mere rhythmic repetition of excitations; rather, a quasi-pleasure consists strictly of an excitation that reproduces the conditions of production of a drive, and thus its determination, along with the determination of pain, is qualitative and not quantitative. A low quantity of excitations or an arrhythmic repetition of excitations is interpreted as quasi-pleasure if it reproduces the conditions of production, but is interpreted as pain if it is antithetical to the conditions of production. A high quantity of excitations or a rhythmic repetition of excitations is interpreted as pain if it is antithetical to the conditions of production, but is interpreted as quasi-pleasure if it reproduces the conditions of production.

<u>The Anti-Production of Fantasy</u>

Deleuze and Guattari mistakenly conceive of an opposition between desiring-machines and the death drive, and conceive of the death drive as the body without organs, as an entity extrinsic to desiring-machines. We critique Deleuze and Guattari's concept at length in our *Science of Self-Actualization* (Kasem 2018, pp. 98-140), and establish that the body without organs is equivalent to the drives constitutive of an organism; we arrive at this conclusion because we reject Kant's theory of the thing-in-itself, following Nietzsche (subtracting all qualia, there is no "thing" left behind), which means that reality, including bodies, consists of psychic forces. Hence the body without organs, which, in our use of the term, refers to the subjectivity of the body, which is constituted by psychic forces. Much of what Deleuze and Guattari write regarding the body without organs applies more to the nature of fantasy, and the relation of fantasies to desiring-machines, and on the other hand, sometimes what they write applies more to the nature of consciousness. To clarify, we conclude in *The Science of Self-Actualization* (ibid) that the body consists of the drives, and we name this concept of the body the body without organs, because we think that this concept of the body without organs is more faithful to the original concept of the body without organs developed by Antonin Artaud, and because it accurately describes the subjectivity of the body. However, in that previous volume we also fundamentally misunderstood the nature of fantasy and the death drive, and we rectify that mistake here.

Freud writes, "Another striking fact is that the life instincts have so much more contact with our internal perception—emerging as breakers of the peace and constantly producing tensions whose release is felt as pleasure—while the death instincts seem to do their work unobtrusively. The pleasure principle seems actually to serve the death instincts. It is true that it keeps watch upon stimuli from without, which are regarded as dangers by both kinds of instincts; but it is more especially on guard against increases of stimulation from within, which would make the task of living more difficult" (1961, p. 57). The pleasure principle appears to effectively serve the death drive because the pleasure principle *is* the death drive. The pleasure principle and the death drive are the negative force of fantasy. All life drives are death drives, all death drives are life drives. The death drive is productive and it is produced. The flows of libido in desiring-machines are flows of death drives. We have outlined above the mechanism whereby fantasy produces the increase of excitations, and thereby produces states of tension of desire, and the mechanism whereby the drives release that tension through an expenditure of energy. Here we shall go into more detail concerning the mechanisms wherein fantasy and desire interact, producing states of tension and releases of tension.

The need of a drive to discharge an excess quantity of excitations, which has its origin internal to the body without organs itself, is driven by the death drive of the pleasure principle, the fantasy of the cessation of excitations. Bataille's general economy of the accursed share characterizes the drives (i.e. their need to discharge their excess, or "accursed share," of energy), but we argue that it is in fact driven by the political economy of the drives, i.e. by the ideological apparatus of a given drive, which by its very nature and function strives to reproduce the conditions of production of a given fantasy. The dramaturgy of the general economy of the accursed share, that is to say, interpreting the general economy of the accursed share according to the motivations of the forces which constitute it, reveals that Bataille's general economy is always already equivalent to the political economy of fantasy, since the need to discharge excess must necessarily have as its motivation the desire to achieve a state of zero intensity, that is to say, a state of pleasure. The discharge of excess excitations is interpreted by a drive to be quasi-pleasure when it means the reproduction of the conditions of production of fantasy. The general economy of the accursed share is the political economy of fantasy in operation.

An apparent conflict arises between raw drive and primary lack because raw drive consists of excitations while simultaneously having primary lack, the complete absence of excitations, as its aim. Because the excitations of raw drive are fundamentally antithetical to the fantasy of primary lack, raw drive's quantity of excitations becomes unbearable to itself and necessitates the discharge of excess excitations. This also applies, mutatis mutandis, to particular drives and their particular fantasies, with their particular contents and forms of life. Fantasy is productive and it is produced, but because it determines the drives as death drives, being the aim of the absolute reduction of excitations, fantasy is also anti-production. Fantasy is not only the object of desire, but also the process of production that produces the object of desire, the activity of fantasizing, but because fantasy is governed by the pleasure principle, it is both the mode of production and the active, dynamic process of anti-production.

Fantasy belongs to both the realms of production and anti-production, and it is via fantasy that production is coupled with anti-production. Fantasy is not a non-productive stasis, but the dynamic and active process of anti-production: the anti-production of production and the production of anti-production. The desiring-machine is defined and determined by the opposition between the dynamic production of the drives and the dynamic anti-production of fantasy.

To paraphrase Deleuze and Guattari (1972/1977, p. 9) for our purposes: In order to resist the excitations of a drive, fantasy presents its smooth, slippery, opaque, taut surface as a barrier. In order to resist a drive's linked, connected, and interrupted flow of excitations, fantasy sets up, and indeed, fantasy *is*, a counterflow of amorphous, undifferentiated fluid. This anti-productive operation of fantasy can only be an operation of primary lack. Primary lack is the element of anti-production inherent in each fantasy. The flow of amorphous, undifferentiated fluid which constitutes an element of fantasy is a flow of primary lack, a flow of pure void.

The Production of Memories

What is memory? It is a drive to remember. We remember only in relation to a fantasy which drives us to remember. We remember both quasi-pleasure and pain only in relation to a fantasy. Previously, we concluded that desiring-machines are best described as multi-valent, active computational modules, meaning that they are intelligent systems capable of sensory integration, associative memory, decision-making, and the control of behaviour. The production of recording, or the encoding of memories, is the process whereby desiring-machines perform sensory integration and produce associative memories, and these processes are in turn integral to decision-making and the control of behaviour.

Fantasy functions as what Deleuze and Guattari (ibid, p. 10) term the *socius* of desiring-production. The socius is the element of anti-production coupled with the productive process (ibid), which in our paradigm means fantasy, the dynamic process of anti-production. On the socius, Deleuze and Guattari (ibid) write, "This is the body that Marx is referring to when he says that it is not the product of labor, but rather appears as its natural or divine presupposition. In fact, it does not restrict itself merely to opposing productive forces in and of themselves. It falls back on (*il se rabat sur*) all production, constituting a surface over which the forces and agents of production are distributed, thereby appropriating for itself all surplus production and arrogating to itself both the whole and parts of the process, which now seem to emanate from it as a quasi-cause. Forces and agents come to represent a miraculous form of its own power: they appear to be "miraculated" (*miracules*) by it. In a word, the socius as a full body forms a surface where all production is recorded, whereupon the entire process appears to emanate from this recording surface." Fantasy is both the product of the unconscious labour of the drives and it is their natural presupposition. Fantasy both drives productive forces, being their aim, and opposes productive forces, since its aim is the total cessation of excitations, and thus the total cessation of all production and productive forces. Fantasy also falls back on (*il se rabat sur*) all desiring-production, constituting a surface over which the forces of production, the psychic forces which are the agents of production, are distributed. Fantasy thereby is not only the mode of production, but also that which appropriates for itself all the surplus production of desiring-production and arrogates to itself both the whole and parts of the process in order to reproduce itself as the mode of production. The surplus production of desiring-production and the whole and the parts of the process of desiring-production therefore emanate from fantasy, which is their cause. Forces, or agents, the psychic forces which *are* agents, are extensions and instruments of the power of fantasy; they are produced by fantasy and they reproduce fantasy. Fantasy, understood as the socius, forms the surface where all desiring-production is recorded, whereupon the entire desiring-production process is reproduced from this recording surface. Fantasy is the page upon which memories are written, and it is from this writing that desiring-production is reproduced. The system Mnem-Ucs (mnemonic unconscious, mnemic unconscious, or memory-unconscious; Freud's term for the unconscious system of memory, which we have revised and which we recognize as an essential component of each desiring-machine or drive) encodes memories only in relation to a fantasy, for it is only in relation to a fantasy that emotional value (which consists of a quantity of excitations inscribed upon a signifying-chain of movement-images; this inscription of a quantity of excitations is also the inscription of a quantity of memorability) is determined. Moreover, the system Mnem-Ucs is not a wholly independent module, but is largely coextensive with desiring-production. That is to say, memories are movement-images in the signifying-chain of desire, and memories are used in desiring-production, both as elements of the mode of production, elements of the objects of desire produced, and as elements of the ideological apparatus, elements of the reproduction of the conditions of production. To understand this metapsychological process in dramaturgical terms: an action's motivation always has, as part of its signifying-chain, primarily unconsciously, what Stanislavski calls an *emotion-memory*. An emotion-memory is a movement-image or sequence of movement-images inscribed with an emotion which is similar to the affect (or command) of the motivation of a given desiring-machine; by the process of association, a motivation recollects a memory which it uses as an emotion-memory, which functions as an affect fused with and strengthening the affect of that motivation. An emotion-memory increases the quantity of affect, or quantity of command, of a motivation. Short-term memory effectively functions as an emotion-memory; the movement-images of perception are immediately inscribed with emotions, according to their relation with the object of desire, and encoded as memories; that is to say, those movement-images are fed back into the signifying-chain of the motivation from which they resulted, and the emotions they have been inscribed with strengthen the affect of the motivation. Long-term memories, too, effectively function as emotion-memories. We call short-term memories those memories which are used as emotion-memories immediately upon their production, whereas we call long-term memories those memories which are used as emotion-memories long after their original production (no doubt they were originally encoded and used as short-term memories), and which are triggered by a process of association, having hitherto been alive within the unconscious as part of a flow of libido within another or the same desiring-machine. All memories are in essence emotion-memories. The function of memory is emotion-memory. Memories are encoded only in order to be used by a desiring-machine to strengthen a motivation, which is simply the automatic process of the encoding of memories; the encoding of memories *is* the production of emotion-memories.

Deleuze and Guattari write that whereas the production of production is characterized by connection, the production of recording is characterized by disjunction (or distribution) (1972/1977, p. 12). When the productive *connections* of desiring-production pass from desiring-machines to fantasy (as capitalist production passes from labour to capital), they then come under the law of *disjunctions*, which expresses *distributions* in relation to the antiproductive function of fantasy, which is metapsychologically the "natural or divine presupposition" (the disjunctions of capital). To paraphrase Deleuze and Guattari for our purposes, desiring-machines attach themselves to fantasy "as so many points of disjunction, between which an entire network of new syntheses is now woven, marking the surface off into coordinates, like a grid. The "either…or…or…or" of the schizophrenic takes over from the "and then"…" (ibid). To continue our paraphrase, no matter what two desiring-machines are involved, the way in which they are attached to the fantasy "must be such that all the disjunctive syntheses between the two amount to the same on the slippery surface. Whereas the "either/or" claims to mark decisive choices between immutable terms (the alternative: either this or that), the schizophrenic "either…or…or" refers to the system of possible permutations between differences that always amount to the same as they shift and slide about" (ibid). The same mode of production, or fantasy, may function as the constant in infinite variations of desiring-machines. Between these infinite variations of desiring-machines an entire network of disjunctive syntheses is woven, marking off the recording-surface of fantasy into coordinates of fantasy, coordinates of desire, like a grid of fantasy, or grid of desire. Considered as a metapsychological entity, the structure of the body without organs is determined by the anti-production of fantasy and its law of disjunctions, which determines the distribution of desiring-machines upon its surface. The production of recording is an activity of the ideological apparatus of a desiring-machine which enables the desiring-machine's mode of production to continue fabricating fantasy-crystals; desiring-machines are all attached to the socius of fantasy as so many ticks upon a warm, blood-filled living body. Fantasy is the life-blood of the body without organs, the fuel of desiring-machines. Fantasy is lack. A socius of fantasy is a socius of lack, an entity of lack; it is lack which is the life-blood of the body without organs, it is lack which fuels desiring-machines, it is lack which is the recording-surface upon which desiring-production is recorded and through which desiring-production is reproduced, it is upon the page of lack that memories are written. A desiring-machine consumes the amorphous, undifferentiated fluid of fantasy, i.e. the amorphous, undifferentiated fluid of lack, and it is with quantities of this fluid of lack, in addition to the flows of libido appropriated and consumed by a desiring-machine from its other connections, that the ideological apparatus of a desiring-machine produces recordings, and these recordings, in turn, are fed back into the mode of production and used to produce fantasy-crystals. The mode of production is not only the production of production, but also the production of anti-production. The relation of disjunction between a desiring-machine and a socius of fantasy is precisely this appropriation-consumption of anti-productive forces by productive forces; the fluid of lack is an anti-productive force which functions as an essential element of productive forces.

Whereas the fluid of libido is measured in quantity of excitations, the fluid of fantasy, which is also the fluid of lack, is measured in potentiality for pleasure. A potentiality for pleasure (potential pleasure or pleasure potential) is a negative quantity which describes the amount of pleasure anticipated. A potentiality for pleasure is not a negative quantity of excitations. Pleasure is a quantity of zero excitations. (We may use the terms "anticipated pleasure" and "pleasure" interchangeably if we keep in mind our definition of pleasure as an imaginary future event which is never experienced). A potentiality of pleasure is a quantity of pleasures, that is to say, it is a quantity of zero excitations, and it is just as purely imaginary as pleasure itself. A potentiality of pleasure begins measurement at the first quantity less than zero, which represents the least potentiality for pleasure; the more negative the quantity, the greater the potentiality for pleasure (e.g. -100 is a greater potentiality for pleasure than -10). The negative quantity of the potentiality for pleasure is in inverse relation to the positive quantity of excitations at any given moment (e.g. -1000 potentiality for pleasure = +1000 excitations). At first glance it may appear paradoxical that the more negative the quantity of potentiality for pleasure, the greater the potentiality for pleasure, since the more negative the quantity the further away it is from the state of zero excitations; however, we have already described this phenomenon above in qualitative terms when we concluded that the state of zero excitations is unachievable in reality and that the higher the quantity of excitations, the greater the strength and peremptoriness of a fantasy, meaning that the greater the quantity of excitations, the greater the potentiality for pleasure, meaning the more negative the quantity of potentiality for pleasure. Furthermore, it may appear that we have described two different phenomena as fantasy, one with a quantity of zero excitations, and the other with any quantity less than zero (the potentiality for pleasure); however, the unit of the latter quantity is not excitations, but zero excitations (e.g. -1000 potentiality for pleasure = -1000 zero excitations). If we simplify the quantity of potential pleasure by multiplying it by its unit, we always arrive at the quantity of zero excitations, for any quantity multiplied by zero is equal to zero, meaning that at bottom our concept of potentiality for pleasure is equivalent to our concept of pleasure, the potential state of zero excitations. Because raw drive and fantasy are inextricable and coextensive, the fluid of lack necessarily implies the presence of raw drive, meaning that when a desiring-machine consumes the fluid of lack from the socius of fantasy, it also consumes the fluid of libido and its quantity of excitations which are inextricable and coextensive with the fluid of lack (i.e. consuming a flow of lack with a quantity of -1000 zero excitations means consuming a flow of libido with a quantity of +1000 excitations). Obversely, consuming a flow of libido means consuming a flow of lack. It is through this mathematics of pleasure that the fluid of lack, an anti-productive force, functions as an essential element of productive forces.

According to Deleuze and Guattari, a desiring-machine is an assemblage of enunciation, which they also alternatively call a rhizome. Recounting Deleuze and Guattari's concept of the assemblage, Adkins writes, "An assemblage is the interconnection of wildly diverse things" (2015, p. 24). In our metapsychology, this means that an assemblage is the interconnection of diverse psychic forces, namely the interconnection between the productive force of the libido and the anti-productive force of fantasy. An assemblage of enunciation is an interlocking complex of different psychic forces which effectively function together as a single module. An assemblage of enunciation is an assemblage of forces, an assemblage of drives, an erotogenic assemblage, and an assemblage of fantasy: an assemblage of actions and an assemblage of motivations. Recounting Deleuze and Guattari's concept of the rhizome, Adkins writes, "Rhizomes do not propagate by way of clearly delineated hierarchies but by underground stems in which any part may send additional shoots upward, downward, or laterally" (ibid, p. 23). Assemblages of forces propagate by underground stems which send additional shoots upward, downward, or laterally to connect with other assemblages. Assemblages of enunciation are rhizomatic assemblages. A rhizomatic assemblage is an intersubjectivity, it is alive and it is a proto-organism. A rhizomatic assemblage is not a discrete, static unity, but a continuous and dynamic system of difference constantly entering into and breaking off combinations among forces. Desiring-machines reproduce themselves in the manner of rhizomes, putting forth shoots and branches out to the furthest corners of the universe.

The grid of desire formed by desiring-machines and the network of disjunctive syntheses between them is a grid consisting of the network of synapses between desiring-machines; the synapses of this network are *assemblage synapses*, or *synapses of affect*. In his book *Schizoanalytic Cartographies*, Guattari briefly mentions the existence of *assemblage synapses* and *synapses of affect* (1989/2013, p. 60). Based upon our own findings as well as Guattari's earlier works co-written with Deleuze, *Anti-Oedipus* and *A Thousand Plateaus*, we develop the concepts *assemblage synapses* and *synapses of affect* in relation to desiring-machines and the production of recording. Desiring-machines are assemblages of enunciation, thus the synapses between desiring-machines are assemblage synapses. Desiring-machines are *semiological neurons*, neurons of semiology, which form *semiological networks* with each other. The signifying chains of desiring-machines use countless signs, often numbering into tens of thousands, and provide for enormous numbers of complex elements of power and switching mechanisms, and includes both complex positive and negative feedback interactions. Such semiological systems parallel, depending on their scale, the capabilities of simple neural network structures as a set of on/off switches with feedback, or complex neural network structures as a set of supercomputers. Regarding computational models of intelligent systems, Trewavas writes, "Even in simple networks collective computational properties arose with parallel processing and extensive numbers of associative memories emerged as attractors occupying part of the network" (2006, p. 5). Semiological networks, whether simple or complex, can be analysed in terms of collective computational properties that arise with parallel processing and extensive numbers of associative memories that emerge as attractors occupying part of the network. All the desiring-machines which constitute a given body without organs participate in the semiological network distributed upon its socius of fantasy; this semiological network is a structure composed of hubs and connectors in which the number of connections to any one desiring-machine obeys a simple power law, meaning that there is a functional relation between the quantity of connections to a given desiring-machine and the quantity of libido in that desiring-machine, wherein a relative change in the quantity of libido of a given desiring-machine results in a proportional relative change in the quantity of connections to other desiring-machines, independent of the initial size of those quantities: the quantity of connections varies as a power of the quantity of libido. These connections between desiring-machines are synapses of affect. Desiring-machines distributed upon a socius of fantasy constantly form and break off rhizomatic connections with each other, and these rhizomatic connections are assemblage synapses, synapses between assemblages. Assemblage synapses are disjunctive connections, they facilitate the exchange of productive and anti-productive forces between desiring-machines. An assemblage synapse is a communication channel between assemblages of enunciation. Although assemblage synapses are initially formed randomly, through the accidental transfer of forces between assemblages, they are subsequently pruned through disuse or strengthened by use. Assemblage synapses function in a manner analogous to neuronal synapses, especially according to the Hebbian theory, which is often summarized by the formula "Cells that fire together wire together," which in more general terms means, as Hebb himself wrote, "The general idea is an old one, that any two cells or systems of cells that are repeatedly active at the same time will tend to become 'associated' so that activity in one facilitates activity in the other" (1949/2002, p. 70). Any two desiring-machines or systems of desiring-machines that are repeatedly active at the same time will tend to become associated so that activity in one facilitates activity in the other. When any two desiring-machines or system of desiring-machines within a body without organs are active at the same time, this increases the likelihood of crosstalk, the accidental transfer of signals, between them, which means that it increases the likelihood of the formation of assemblage synapses; and once these synapses are formed, they are strengthened, the effectivity of communication is increased, when they are active at the same time on further occasions. Desiring-machines that produce together, reproduce together in the manner of rhizomes. To phrase it another way, desiring-machines that crystallize together, build ties together. The rhizomatic connection of an assemblage synapse is a rhizomatic disjunction, a disjunctive synthesis, it is a module whose function is the production of recording. In other words, assemblage synapses between desiring-machines plays a role in the formation of memories. The strength of two connected metapsychological pathways results in the dynamic longevity of emotion-memories, and thus the storage of information. Assemblage synapses are synapses of emotion-memories and synapses of affect, entities of motivational facilitation, entities that facilitate a motivation, as well as entities that facilitate the pragmatic manifestation of a motivation. Via an assemblage synapse, desiring-machines exchange quantities of libido, which means they exchange quantities of fantasy, i.e. quantities of lack; the quantity of libido is also a signifying-chain which includes in it motivation, fantasy, lack, and emotion-memories. Because a desiring-machine is an assemblage of motivation, it is an assemblage of affect, and thus assemblage synapses are synapses of affect, since they facilitate the intensity and pragmatic manifestation of an affect, meaning that assemblage synapses increase the peremptoriness of the command of a drive and thus increase a drive's pragmatic manifestation.

Excitation is semiotic and illocutionary, excitations exist only as forms of action and forms of inscription. Excitations inscribe memories in disjunction with the anti-productive forces of fantasy, and this process of the production of recording may also be called, following Deleuze and Guattari, *disjunctive inscription*. The language of excitations, potentialities for pleasure, and movement-images is the programming language with which the algorithms constitutive of the organism are written; we shall more simply call this language the *language of affects*. The code of the unconscious is written in the language of affects. Signifying-chains of the language of affects form unambiguous specifications for performing calculations, data-processing, automated reasoning, machine learning, and other tasks. (There are different "logics" in the psyche dependent upon which algorithm is running, i.e. which force is dominant). As an effective method, a method for solving a problem from a specific class, a psychical algorithm can be expressed within a finite amount of space and time in the language of affects, which is well-defined with respect to the agent, the mental apparatus, that executes the psychical algorithm, for calculating a function. Starting from an initial psychical state and initial psychosemiotic input, the instructions (written in the language of affects) proceeds through a finite number of well-defined successive psychical states, eventually producing psychosemiotic output and terminating at a final ending psychical state. The transition from one psychical state to the next is not necessarily deterministic; some algorithms, known as randomized psychical algorithms, incorporate random psychosemiotic input. The energy of disjunctive inscription is the same kind of energy that powers the psyche, libido. The anti-productive process of fantasy coupled with the production of recording makes the socius of fantasy, regardless of what the content of the fantasy may be, appear as if divine. It is not only the case that God is a fantasy. The fantasy is God. The fantasy is the fetish in both the sexual and the religious sense. Memory is always the index of a desire.

The Production of Consciousness

All the psychic processes we have described thus far are primarily unconscious. Consciousness is merely the accidental by-product, the epiphenomenon, of unconscious psychic processes; or, to phrase it another way, consciousness is the surplus value of unconscious desiring-production. The third productive process of desiring-production, the production of consumptions, yields consciousness. The production of consumptions is the production of consciousness. As we concluded in *The Science of Self-Actualization*, perception, the appropriation and consumption of qualia, is an activity of the system Ucs (the system unconscious), thus we described the module of perception as the system Pcpt-Ucs (the system perception-unconscious) (Kasem 2018, pp. 170-174; ibid, pp. 190-199); we amend our discovery here, recognizing that each desiring-machine has a system Pcpt-Ucs module, just as each desiring-machine has a system Mnem-Ucs module. (Following Freud, we also describe consciousness as the system Cs, or system consciousness, although our account of consciousness differs significantly from Freud's). Unconscious perceptions are primary; consciousness is not perception, but the surplus value of unconscious perceptions. That is to say, "reality," our perception of and connection with the external world, is primarily unconscious, and the "reality" experienced by consciousness is merely the surplus value of the unconscious and its interactions with a likewise unconscious "reality." We call the environment, which consists of unconscious psychic forces, the *Real* or *proto-Real*, and we call the experience of consciousness *reality*, even though it is in fact the hallucination of the surplus value of desiring-production. Lacan makes a conceptual distinction between the Real and reality. The Real, as we wrote above, is that from which the object of desire is wholly absent. Reality, on the other hand, is that which is mediated by fantasy, i.e. that which is mediated by the object of desire; in other words, the reality experienced by consciousness is experienced only in relation to fantasy and the possibility of satisfying desire, i.e. the possibility of experiencing pleasure. In our metapsychology, reality is consciousness, and it is produced by the system Ucs via the production of consumption. The external world is the Real, that from which the object of desire is wholly absent. We also describe the external world as proto-Real in order to indicate that it cannot be reduced merely by language alone, although language may obscure it, thus differentiating our concept of the Real from Lacan's (which can be reduced by language). The proto-Real is the Real which exists beneath the Lacanian Real.

Deleuze and Guattari write, "Conforming to the meaning of the word "process," recording falls back on (*se rabat sur*) production, but the production of recording itself is produced by the production of production. Similarly, recording is followed by consumption, but the production of consumption is produced in and through recording" (1972/1977, p. 16). Previously, we concluded that the nature of memory is essentially that of the emotion-memory, meaning that the production of recording is the production of emotion-memories. The memories produced by the production of recording are fed back into desiring-production and its mode of production, but the memories were produced in the first place as a result of desiring-production and its mode of production. Similarly, although the production of consumption, as the production of surplus value, follows the production of recording, the production of consumption is produced in the first place in and through the production of recording. The production of memories is at one and the same time the production of emotions because both processes occur together in the same process of production that is the production of emotion-memories. It is the production of surplus emotion-memories that defines the production of consumption as the production of emotions as such. The failure to possess the object of desire results in the production of memories, and it is the inevitable exponential intensification of the failure to possess the object of desire, a process as inevitable as the initial failure to possess the object of desire, that results in the accumulation of surplus memories which all have as their content the failure to possess the object of desire and the feeling of this failure, and it is the surplus of this feeling that defines emotion as such. Emotion is always already surplus emotion because emotion is defined by its very existence as surplus. Consciousness is produced by this very surplus of emotion, consciousness *is* this very surplus of emotion; consciousness is the awareness born of the feeling of the failure to possess the object of desire. Moreover, the movement-images which constitute short-term memories serve as the matter from which the reality of consciousness is hallucinated. It is in this sense that desiring-machines are hallucination-machines. The surplus value of emotion-memories, which means the surplus value of movement-images as well as the surplus-value of emotions, constitutes consciousness.

Above, we mentioned the finding of Stanislavski that emotions result naturally from motivations. However, how do emotions result naturally from motivations? And what exactly are emotions? Motivations in themselves do not produce emotions; rather, motivations produce emotions only in relation to a degree of conflict. Because conflict is immanent, motivations always occur in scenarios of conflict, and thus emotions always result from motivations. On the one hand, a motivation always experiences conflicts, or resistances or obstacles, in its quest to possess its object of desire. On the other hand, a motivation also experiences obstacles, and thus conflicts, in its quest to reproduce the conditions of its mode of production. Whereas the former type of conflict is systemic and perpetual, since the object of desire is wholly absent from the proto-Real, the latter type of conflict is systemic but not perpetual, it is relieved when the system Pcpt-Ucs of a drive appropriates and consumes the qualia necessary for its conditions of production (quasi-pleasures). However, both types of conflict result in states of tension for the drive, tension between the drive's demand to satisfy itself and the resistances to its satisfaction, and these states of tension are emotions. A quasi-pleasure, although it satisfies a drive's need to reproduce its conditions of production, is nonetheless also a state of tension, since it is also a failure to possess the object of desire.

Because a quantity of libido is a quantity of intensity and desiring-machines consist of quantities of libido, desiring-machines consist of quantities of intensity, or intensive quantities, flows of intensity and interruptions of flows of intensity. Because the energy which flows through, determines, and animates the system Cs is the libido, the system Cs also consists of intensive quantities. Intensive quantities are states of tension. The states of tension that define consciousness are different from the states of tension that define unconscious desiring-machines in that consciousness is the surplus value of states of tension, the surplus value of intensive states, which have resulted from unconscious desiring-production. States of tension are quantities of tension. States of tension are states of unpleasure, or states of pain, since they consist of a quantity of excitations and true pleasure would consist of a state of zero excitations (zero intensity, or zero tension). Even "joy," "pleasure," and "happiness," as they are named in everyday language, are in fact merely states of quasi-pleasure, since they consist of excitations, which means that they too consist of states of pain. Even self-enjoyment is a form of suffering, a surplus of suffering. Every quantity of excitations, because it is a positive quantity of excitations above zero excitations, is pain, a quantity of pain-excitations.

Consciousness is narcissistic. Freud writes, "It is hard to say anything of the behaviour of the libido in the id and in the super-ego. All that we know about it relates to the ego, in which at first the whole available quota of libido is stored up. We call this state the absolutely primary narcissism. It lasts till the ego begins to cathect the ideas of objects with libido, to transform narcissistic libido into object-libido. Throughout the whole of life the ego remains the great reservoir, from which libidinal cathexes are sent out to objects and into which they are also once more withdrawn, just as an amoeba behaves with its pseudopodia" (1960, p. 69). Although we reject, for the most part, Freud's topographical model, as well as Freud's concept of the ego, he here makes a pertinent observation on the nature of consciousness. Following Nietzsche's discovery that the ego is merely a linguistic construct, a fiction of language, and William James's discovery that consciousness is in fact a stream-of-consciousness, we recognize that consciousness is a system of difference, mediation, becoming, and multiplicity. However, when Freud here writes of the ego, he refers to consciousness, and his conclusion that consciousness is characterized by primary narcissism applies to consciousness even when consciousness is considered as a system of difference, mediation, becoming, and multiplicity. The behaviour of the libido in the system Ucs is not accessible to direct observation, and so must be inferred. However, the behaviour of the libido in the system Cs is directly observable, at least considering one's own system Cs; the behaviour of the libido in the system Cs of the other is not directly observable and must also be inferred. Freud writes that the system Cs is the great reservoir of libido, the storage tank of libido and the source of libido supply. It is this function of the system Cs as the reservoir of libido that characterizes it as a system of primary narcissism. Freud writes that the system Cs cathects and withdraws quantities of libido from objects because he mistakenly equates consciousness with the perception of the external world and the external world with objectality. In actuality, it is the unconscious which perceives the external world, which consists of psychic forces; objectality is a quality of ideas fabricated by the drives, beginning with the first fabrication, the object of desire. It is the system Pcpt-Ucs that cathects and withdraws libido from the environment, and it is the system Mnem-Ucs that cathects and withdraws libido from the fabricated ideas we mistakenly call "objects." The drives of the system Ucs are characterized by essential narcissism because their primary function is to satisfy themselves; however, they also exist, and always already exist, connected to and in relation with the other psychic forces that constitute their environment, and it is this connection and relation with the external world and the Real that guarantees both the perpetual dissatisfaction of the drives and the realism of the drives. The realism of the drives is the non-narcissism of the drives, their connection and relationship with something other than themselves and fantasy, i.e. their connection and relationship with the Real; to borrow Heidegger's concept, this is the *thrownness* of the unconscious, its originary quality of being thrown into the world like a pair of dice. However, throughout the entirety of the life of an organism, consciousness remains cut off from the external world and from the Real, that is to say, consciousness remains narcissistically self-enclosed, and it is this narcissistic self-enclosement, the primary narcissism of consciousness, which makes consciousness the great reservoir of libido.

The primary narcissism of consciousness is reflected in the metaphysical problems of the ego as they are described by rationalist philosophers. In his *Meditations* (2010), Descartes argues that the existence of the ego is the fundamental truth of existence. Descartes is not a solipsist, although he does touch upon the fact that if we accept his argument that the existence of the ego is an incontrovertible truth, solipsism appears at first glance to be the only viable philosophy, since the existence of the ego is true without a doubt, whereas the existence of an external world is open to doubt; Descartes escapes this quandary, at least initially, by noting that although the existence of the external world is dubitable, it is not for that reason alone false. Descartes writes that all perceptions, meaning all conscious perceptions, consist of qualities, and since qualities are not, strictly speaking, objective, but are dependent upon subjective perceptions and thus dependent upon subjectivity (e.g. the concept of colour makes no sense independent of subjectivity), the only certain knowledge we glean from conscious perceptions is the existence of the ego. Thus we have two related metaphysical problems which are explicated by Descartes, although they are far older than Descartes: the problem of solipsism and the problem of the thing-in-itself. The problem of solipsism is, "Does anything exist independent of my own ego?" The problem of the thing-in-itself is, "Does there exist a thing-in-itself, a thing devoid of qualities, which would constitute, if it existed, the external world, that is to say, the world independent of my own ego?" It is evident that these are at bottom the same problem, the problem of solipsism. We address these problems at length in terms of metaphysics in *The Science of Self-Actualization* (Kasem 2018). Here, we observe that these metaphysical problems arise only from the limited perspective of consciousness, which is limited to perceiving only the qualia constitutive of consciousness, which means that consciousness is limited to perceiving only itself. The existence of the unconscious can never be directly perceived, but only inferred with the use of reason, for example, from the fact of the involuntary generation of emotions. That the thing-in-itself does not exist and that the external world actually consists of psychic forces is likewise an inference of reason; it is outlined by Nietzsche in *Beyond Good and Evil* and *The Twilight of the Idols*, and recounted by us in *The Science of Self-Actualization* (cf. Kasem 2018, pp. 98-140). Descartes believes he proves that the fundamental truth of existence is the existence of the ego ("I think therefore I am"), but what he actually proves, inadvertently, is the narcissistic self-enclosement of consciousness, which knows and perceives only itself, hence the primary narcissism of consciousness.

Consciousness is a *system* (hence the *system* Cs), which means that it consists of elements that function together as a whole in order to produce an effect. The elements of consciousness are the psychic forces which constitute it. The system Cs consists of the surplus of emotion-memories, that is to say, it is the direct result of the production of recording and is produced in and through the production of recording, which means that the system Cs is the surplus value of the system Mnem-Ucs. In other words, the system Cs is a module of the ideological apparatus of the psyche, since it is produced in and through the system Mnem-Ucs, which is an essential component the ideological apparatus of the system Ucs. The system Cs, as a module of the body without organs, has a relative autonomy, although it is determined in the last instance by the system Ucs. Consciousness is an organ of the body. The function of the system Cs is to store the surplus value of libido produced by the system Ucs and to supply the system Ucs with a source of libido. Conscious does not make decisions, nor does it reason, and it certainly has no free will, for it is the unconscious which makes decisions and it is the unconscious which reasons, and free will simply does not exist; the unconscious is the primary active agent of the psyche, and consciousness is merely a reservoir of psychic energy.

The system Cs can be discerned on the recording-surface of the unconscious, wandering about over the socius of fantasy. To paraphrase Deleuze and Guattari for our purposes (1972/1977, p. 16), the system Cs always remains "peripheral to the desiring-machines, being defined by the share of the product it takes for itself, garnering here, there and everywhere a reward in the form of a becoming or an avatar, being born of the states that it consumes and being reborn with each new state. "It's me, and so it's mine…" Even suffering, as Marx says, is a form of self-enjoyment. Doubtless all desiring-production is, in and of itself, immediately consumption and consummation, and therefore, "sensual pleasure."" The system Cs is the consumption-consummation of desiring-production, the "sensual pleasure" of desiring-production. The system Cs is always peripheral to the processes of desiring-production, that is to say, it is always peripheral to the system Ucs. The system Ucs determines and defines the system Cs by the excess share of libido, the surplus value of libido, it transfers to the system Cs. These accursed shares of subjectivity have varying contents, hence why the system Cs is reborn with each new state. The system Cs is the surplus value of the system Ucs, the surplus value of desiring-production, which means that it is the epiphenomenon, the random byproduct and residuum, of desiring-production. This residuum of desiring-production is jouissance. Consciousness is the immediate and coextensive consumption-consummation of desiring-production, which means that consciousness is the jouissance of desiring-production. Jouissance is the surplus increase of the quantity of excitations, or the surplus quantity of excitations. Jouissance is always already surplus jouissance, since it is always already the accursed share of excitations, and thus the accursed share of jouissance. Consciousness is jouissance, jouissance is consciousness. Jouissance can take many different forms depending on the content which defines it. Not only quasi-pleasure, but also pain, suffering, sadness, anger, fear, grief, and misery are all forms of jouissance. All emotions are forms of jouissance. Jouissance is enjoyment, which always means self-enjoyment. Jouissance is the surplus value of excitations, which means that is the surplus value of pain-excitations. In other words, jouissance is always the jouissance of pain, the surplus of pain. Self-enjoyment is simultaneously a form of suffering and the enjoyment of suffering. The stream of consciousness is the surplus of libido produced by unconscious desiring-production; the stream of consciousness is a reservoir of libido which, upon its production, functions as the supply source of libido for unconscious desiring-production which is internal to the body without organs, meaning that the stream of consciousness is drained off and used up by unconscious desiring-production; thus, the fluid of consciousness, the fluid of libido which constitutes the stream of consciousness, is accounted for, both in terms of how this fluid is produced and where this fluid goes after it has been produced. The stream of consciousness does not mysteriously vanish into nothingness, nor does it endlessly accumulate, but rather, it is drained off by unconscious desiring-machines and thus recycled for use in unconscious desiring-production.

The libido is used in the production of production as the energy of production, in the production of recording the libido is used as the energy of recording, and in the production of consumption the libido is used as the energy of consummation. To paraphrase Deleuze and Guattari, surplus libido, or residual libido, is "the motive force behind the third synthesis of the unconscious: the conjunctive synthesis "so it's…", or the production of consumption" (1972/1977, p. 17). The conjunctive synthesis is formed and consciousness is produced by the accumulation of surplus libido, that is to say, the accumulation of surplus intensive states. To paraphrase Deleuze and Guattari (ibid, pp. 17-18), consciousness is the experience of this third productive machine, consumption, and the "residual reconciliation it brings about: a conjunctive synthesis of consummation in the form of a wonderstruck "So *that's* what it was!"" The accumulation of surplus intensive states constitutive of the conjunctive synthesis of consummation is the production of emotion; emotion is always already this surplus of intensive states, meaning that emotion is always already surplus emotion, in the same way that jouissance is always already surplus jouissance. The jouissance at the core of consciousness, which is the core of consciousness no matter the particular content of consciousness, since consciousness, regardless of its content, is always surplus jouissance, it is always implicitly the wonderstruck feeling "So *that's* what it was!", "So it's…", and "It's me, and so it's mine…".

Consciousness *is* the conjunctive synthesis. How exactly is the conjunctive synthesis formed? Or what amounts to the same thing, how exactly is the surplus of intensive states accumulated? To answer this question, we must take into account the three forms of production (the production of production, the production of recording, and the production of consumption), their corresponding entities (desiring-machines, the socius of fantasy, and consciousness), and their interrelations. A conflict arises between the production of desiring-machines and the anti-production of fantasy. To paraphrase Deleuze and Guattari (ibid, p. 9), every coupling of a desiring-machine, every sound of a desiring-machine running, becomes unbearable to consciousness; beneath its organs, consciousness senses there are larvae and loathsome worms, and a God at work messing it all up or strangling it by organizing it; for consciousness, the productive forces of desire are merely so may nails piercing the flesh, so many forms of torture. The production of desiring-machines and their positive quantities of excitations (the will to power) is the *attraction* of desiring-machines to the anti-production of fantasy and its negative quantity of zero excitations (the potentialities for pleasure), whereas the anti-production of fantasy and its negative quantity of zero excitations is the *repulsion* of desiring-machines and their positive quantities of excitations by the socius of fantasy and its quantity of zero excitations. The surplus quantities of tension which define consciousness are produced by the attraction and repulsion of desiring-machines and fantasy. Quantities of tension are not in opposition to each other, nor do they ever arrive at a state of balance around a neutral state. Quantities of tension are all positive quantities in relation to the zero tension and zero intensity of fantasy. To paraphrase Deleuze and Guattari for our purposes, quantities of tension undergo increases or decreases "depending on the complex relationship between them and the variations in the relative strength of attraction and repulsion as determining factors" (ibid, p. 19). As Deleuze and Guattari (ibid) write, "the opposition of the forces of attraction and repulsion produces an open series of intensive elements," the quantities of tension, "all of them positive, that are never an expression of the final equilibrium of a system." We add that quantities of tension consist of dynamic, unstable states (these dynamic, unstable states are the states of tension), the surplus of which constitutes consciousness. The surplus of dynamic, unstable states of tension is the open series of states of subjectivity, or mental states, that defines the stream of consciousness. The attraction and repulsion of desiring-machines and fantasy produce states of tension, which are intense *nervous states* or intensive quantities; intensive quantities are filled up to varying degrees with the fluid of lack, and these intensive quantities in turn fill up to varying degrees the body without organs, without ever significantly filling up the negative space, or void, of primary lack. The greater the strength of attraction, the higher the quantity of intensity that results; the greater the strength of repulsion, the higher the quantity of intensity that results. Furthermore, at any given time, attraction and repulsion are in a relationship either of positive feedback or negative feedback with each other. When attraction and repulsion are in a relationship of positive feedback, an increase in the strength of attraction results in the increase of the strength of repulsion and vice versa, and this positive feedback cycle also results in the production of higher quantities of intensity. When attraction and repulsion are in a relationship of negative feedback, a decrease in the strength of attraction results in the decrease of the strength of repulsion and vice versa, and this negative feedback cycle also results in the production of lower quantities of intensity. The proportions of attraction and repulsion between desiring-machines and fantasy produce, starting from a quantity greater than zero, a series of quantities tension, or states of tension, as surplus value; consciousness is born of each surplus state of tension in the series, and consciousness is continually reborn by the following state of tension that determines it at a given moment; the system Cs is the consumption-consummation of all these surplus states of tension, which are also surplus excitations, that cause the stream of consciousness to be born and reborn.

The system Cs is an egg. Deleuze and Guattari invent a profound and idiosyncratic concept, the *egg*, as a metaphor for lived experience. However, they mistakenly identify the egg of lived experience with their concept of the body without organs, which is akin to Freud's death drive, a death drive separate from the life drives. Not only do we recognize the essential fusion of the death drive and the life drive, and not only do we conceive of the body without organs as the entire subjectivity of the body, including within itself both desiring-machines, the socius of fantasy, and the system Cs, but we also identify consciousness as the true egg of lived experience. To paraphrase Deleuze and Guattari (ibid, p. 19) for our purposes, the egg of consciousness is "crisscrossed with axes and thresholds, with latitudes and longitudes and geodesic lines, traversed by *gradients* marking the transitions and the becomings, the destinations of the subject along these particular vectors. Nothing here is representative; rather, it is all life and lived experience: the actual, lived emotion of having breasts does not resemble breasts, it does not represent them, any more than a predestined zone in the egg resembles the organ that it is going to be stimulated to produce within itself. Nothing but bands of intensity, potentials, thresholds, and gradients." Reality, the reality of lived experience, is the egg of consciousness. Reality is the surplus value of unconscious desiring-production. Reality, the lived experience of consciousness, its perception-images and cognitions, consists of the movement-images and emotions that constitute the content of the surplus excitations of desiring-production. Reality is the surplus hallucination of the unconscious, reality is always already surplus reality, always already surreality, in the same way that jouissance is always already surplus jouissance. The egg of consciousness is the egg of reality. Reality consists of qualia, which are quanta of subjective experience. Qualia are the qualities, or qualitative states, that constitute the reality experienced by consciousness (e.g. the particular colour of a particular "thing" at a given time is a quale). The qualia constitutive of reality consist of bands of intensity, potentials (viz. potentialities for pleasure), thresholds, transitions, becomings, and gradients which are the indices of transitions and becomings. Qualia are not in themselves representations. Qualia are quanta of lived experience, in other words, qualia *are* lived experience. Qualia are the actual, lived emotions constitutive of the perception-images and cognitions of lived experience. Reality is crisscrossed with axes and thresholds of emotions, with latitudes and longitudes and geodesic lines of emotions, traversed by gradients indexing the transitions of emotions and the becomings of lived experience.

The Three Forms of Libido

To recapitulate, the body without organs consists of three types of production, their corresponding three passive syntheses, their corresponding three dramaturgical modules, their corresponding three types of machines, and their corresponding three forms of energy, all of which function together as a whole to constitute the life of the organism. We have derived our economic model of the body largely from Deleuze and Guattari's *Anti-Oedipus*, making modifications to their theories in order to account for the findings of other psychologists, most notably Leopardi, Stanislavski, Proust, Stendhal, Nietzsche, Lacan, and Freud, and thereby constructing a synthesis of all of their findings. We have included in this and previous sections the extensive citations for what we here recapitulate.

The three types of production are the production of production, the production of recording, and the production of consumption. Their corresponding three types of passive syntheses are the connective syntheses, the disjunctive syntheses, and the conjunctive syntheses. These three passive syntheses constitute the what Deleuze and Guattari term "the autoproduction of the unconscious" (ibid, p. 26), the automatic productive processes, or automatic writing, that constitute the unconscious. Stanislavski constructed his method of acting by reverse-engineering the psyche, and he recorded his method as a science, an organized and useful body of knowledge; we have reconstructed Stanislavski's metapsychology by analysing his science of acting and applying it to the observation and analysis of humans in their "natural" environment, that is to say, in the field or *in natura*, and we have modified it in order to account for the findings of the researchers mentioned above. We have concluded that there are three main dramaturgical modules that compose the psyche (motivation, memory, and emotion), and that these three dramaturgical modules are autoproduced and that they constitute the autoproduction of the unconscious. The production of production, or the connective syntheses, is the production of motivation. The production of recording, or the disjunctive syntheses, is the production of memory. The production of consumption, or the conjunctive syntheses, is the production of emotion.

In order to more accurately describe the three types of machines as we conceive of them, we have given them different names than the names given them by Deleuze and Guattari. The three corresponding entities of the three types of production are desiring-machines (the production of production), the socius of fantasy (the production of recording), and consciousness (the production of consumption). Each of these entities is a type of machine, a system of flows and interruptions of flows. Desiring-machines are *masochistic machines*. We may also describe desiring-machines, along with Deleuze and Guattari, as "organ-machines," but in their relationship with the socius of fantasy, desiring-machines embody the pathology of masochism, hence they are masochistic machines. Desire is masochistic because it yields only pain for the subject of desire. Unconscious desiring-machines are the subject of desire and desire is perpetual pain, hence why we describe desiring-machines as masochistic machines. The socius of fantasy is the *lack-machine*. We may also describe the socius, along with Deleuze and Guattari, as the "miraculating machine," that which miraculates, reproduces and causes, desiring-production, but only if we keep in mind that the socius of fantasy *is* lack, meaning that the socius is primarily a lack-machine, and it is only on the basis of its existence as lack that the socius miraculates, reproduces and causes, desiring-production. Consciousness is the *sensual machine*. Desire is sensuality, and consciousness is sensual in a multifold sense: consciousness is the residuum of sensuality, consciousness is the reservoir of sensuality, consciousness is in part constituted by sensations which are themselves the residua of sensuality, and consciousness is the emotion which results from sensuality, meaning that consciousness is the emotion of sensuality and thus in a sense it is the feeling of sensuality, the sensuality of sensuality.

Freud wrote that there are two forms of energy, free energy and bound energy, and Nietzsche similarly proposed that there are two forms of force, active force and reactive force; however, we have discovered that all energy is free energy and that all force is active force. Because force and energy are one and the same phenomenon, we may also say that all force is free force and that all energy is active energy. Freud conceived of free energy as energy which tends towards immediate and total discharge, whereas he conceived of bound energy as energy which is blocked from discharging. Free energy is mobile and capable of discharge, whereas bound energy is immobile, static, and incapable of discharge. Free energy is mobile cathexis, whereas bound energy is immobile cathexis. However, Nietzsche had earlier discovered that "every power draws its ultimate consequences at every moment" (BGE, 22), meaning that the very function of energy is to discharge itself, that is to say, energy is defined by its discharge; each quanta of psychic energy fully actualizes its full potential at each given moment of its existence. In other words, there is no bound energy. All energy is free energy: mobile, capable of discharge, and tending towards immediate and total discharge. All cathexis of energy is mobile cathexis. However, Nietzsche's own discovery that all energy is free energy also means Nietzsche's distinction between active forces and reactive forces is a false one, and that all forces are active forces. We summarized Nietzsche's distinction between active forces and reactive forces, which we also call active drives and reactive drives, earlier in *The Science of Self-Actualization* (Kasem 2018, pp. 199-200): "Nietzsche writes that active drives are essentially spontaneous, aggressive, expansive, form-giving forces, whereas reactive drives are essentially adaptative forces; the adaptations of the reactive drives follow only after the spontaneous activity of the active drives (GM, II, 12). The active drives are the drives which essentially reach out for power. Deleuze writes that the essential activities of the active drives are "appropriating, possessing, subjugating, dominating" (1962/1983, p. 42). Deleuze further explicates, "To appropriate means to impose forms, to create forms by exploiting circumstances" (ibid). The appropriations performed by active drives are only possible via the discharge of their excess strength; this discharge of excess strength is precisely the spontaneous imposition of "forms." The exploitation of circumstances by the active drives is also the creation of new "forms" because the active drives exploit circumstances only via discharging their (the active drives') own-most excess strength." An active force's discharge of its own-most strength is the discharge of the quantity of energy which constitutes it. That is to say, active force is free energy, free energy is active force. The spontaneity of active forces is precisely their discharge of the quantity of energy internal to them outward into the external world. Active forces act from out of themselves, never merely as a reaction to stimuli. Nietzsche never clearly explicates how exactly active force, which he clearly identifies with the will to power, is transformed into reactive force, which only ever reacts to stimuli and never acts spontaneously from out of itself. We argue that all forces are active forces because all forces tend towards immediate and total discharge. Moreover, we may also conceive of the distinction between active and reactive forces in terms of Chomsky's critique of behaviourism, outlined in his essay "A Review of B. F. Skinner's *Verbal Behavior*" (1959). Chomsky reproached Skinner's behaviourism for conceiving of the human psyche solely in terms of reactions to stimuli, which Chomsky argued was a deficient psychological theory because it failed to account for creative and spontaneous human activity; for example, language. Chomsky writes that Skinner accounts for language in terms of "verbal behaviour," that is to say, in terms of reactions to stimuli, but his theory of "verbal behaviour" fails to account for the production of new sentences performed by all language users, even by children who have just learned how to speak. We argue that only the existence and dominance of active forces in each and every psyche accounts for creative activity, such as for example, the production of new sentences, because only active forces have the capacity for spontaneity and creativity necessary for the creative act, the production of the new. If reactive forces were capable of dominating the psyche, such that we could refer to a "reactive type" of psyche, then such a human being with a "reactive type" of psyche would perfectly embody Skinner's behaviourism, and as a result, would only be capable of "verbal behaviour," and would be thoroughly incapable of doing something as simple as producing new sentences. Even computer programs are capable of producing new sentences. Creativity is not inherently virtuous, nor is there anything special merely in the production of the new, since all organisms are creative and are capable of producing the new, even parasites and fascists. As painful as such a conclusion may be to one's pride, even the man of ressentiment is capable of the creative act (e.g. Richard Wagner, Leni Riefenstahl, and Alfred Rosenberg), which means that even ressentiment is an active drive, and to treat it medically it must be analysed as such. We conclude that there are no reactive forces whatsoever because it is evident that active forces predominate in each and every psyche, which means that supposing the existence of reactive forces is completely useless and superfluous. Therefore, the Libido is always a form of free energy—mobile, capable of discharge, and tending towards immediate and total discharge, performing mobile cathexes—and a form of active force—spontaneous, aggressive, expansive, and creative—and all forms of Libido are likewise forms of free energy and active force.

Deleuze and Guattari write that the psychic energy of the unconscious is converted into three different forms in order to serve as the motive forces of the three different passive syntheses: the energy of the connective syntheses is *Libido*, which is converted into *Numen* to function as the motive force of the disjunctive syntheses, and is then converted into *Voluptas* to function as the motive force of the conjunctive syntheses (ibid, pp. 16-17). We amend their discovery here based on the fact that these different types of energy are different types of the same energy, namely the Libido, and to distinguish the energy of the connective syntheses, we name the energy of the connective syntheses the *Will-to-Power* (after Nietzsche's concept of the will to power, since desiring-machines perform the function Nietzsche ascribes to the will to power, appropriating and consuming forces from the environment). Moreover, we have discovered one other form of Libido, namely Raw Drive, and we have discovered a form of negative energy, or anti-productive energy, in the unconscious (as opposed to the positive energy, or productive energy, of the Libido), which we have sometimes called Lack, and at other times called Fantasy and Primary Lack. Lack and Libido are two very different forms of psychic energy which coexist in the unconscious, although they are inseparable from and coextensive with each other, and reciprocally increase each other in a positive feedback loop (except when the body is dying, in which case they reciprocally decrease each other in a negative feedback loop). Will-to-Power is the labour force of desiring-production and it is the connective labour of desiring-machines. We may also describe desiring-machines as *power-machines*, as in Will-to-Power-machines. We describe the Libido in terms of three different forms of energy because the Libido performs three different functions at each stage of the process of desiring-production. The Libido is a system of energy, meaning that it consists of elements which function together to produce an effect. The three different functions of the Libido are three different effects, and from them we can infer three different systems of energy which have produced them. Each transformation of the Libido is a systemic change, or structural change, a change in the very structure of the energy of Libido, and it is three very different structures of Libido that produce the aforementioned three different effects. (The question of what exactly the elements of Libido are, and what exactly are the relations between these elements that constitute the three different structures of Libido, are both very pertinent questions to psychoanalysis, the inquiry into which will likely prove very fruitful, but which is beyond the scope of the present work). The three different functions of Libido are the three different passive syntheses of desiring-production: the connective syntheses, the disjunctive syntheses, and the conjunctive syntheses. Each form of passive synthesis implies a different structure of Libido which performs that synthesis. In the connective syntheses, the function of the Libido is the appropriation-consumption of other psychic forces. The Will-to-Power functions as the motive force of the connective syntheses of desiring-production. In the disjunctive syntheses, the function of the Libido is the inscription of memories. When the Will-to-Power is transformed into Numen, Numen functions as the motive force of the disjunctive syntheses of the production of recording. Numen is the energy of disjunctive inscription (ibid, p. 13). Numen is the form of Libido which inscribes memories in disjunction with the anti-productive forces of the socius of fantasy. Numen is the Libido which is inseparable from and coextensive with the fluid of lack, or anti-productive force, constitutive of the socius of fantasy. Numen is the libidinal energy which flows through the socius of fantasy, the socius of fantasy which appears divine because it attracts to itself the desiring-machines and thus the entire process of desiring-production, and because it serves as the enchanted, miraculating surface of desiring-production, inscribing itself into each and every one of its disjunctions with desiring-machines. As we wrote above, the fantasy is God, the sexual fetish and religious fetish of desire. The excitations which inscribe memories are quantities of Libido in the form of Numen, or quantities of Numen. In the conjunctive syntheses, the function of the Libido is to be the reservoir of Libido, the storage tank and supply source of Libido, for the unconscious. When part of the energy of recording (Numen) is transformed into Voluptas, Voluptas functions as the motive force of the conjunctive syntheses of the production of consumption. Voluptas is the energy of consumption-consummation.

     The Libido is transformed into different types of energy due to the ever-increasing degree of strength of the attraction and repulsion between desiring-machines and the socius of fantasy, which tends to increase in a positive feedback cycle except when the organism is dying, in which case it tends to decrease in a negative feedback cycle. As the degree of strength of attraction and repulsion between desiring-machines and the socius of fantasy accumulates, the quantities of tension in the Libido accumulate, and this increase of quantities of tension results first in the conversion of Will-to-Power into Numen, and then as the increase of quantities of tension continues it results in the conversion of Numen into Voluptas.

Voluptas is redistributed into the libidinal economy of desiring-production via being appropriated-consumed by the desiring-machines which began the process of desiring-production; when Voluptas is appropriated-consumed by the desiring-machines, it is converted back into Will-to-Power by the very process of being appropriated-consumed, and is then subsequently used as part of the labour force of the connective syntheses. Each transformation of energy is the means by which each corresponding type of machine is produced, and the function of each form of energy is what each corresponding type of machine produces. The lack-machine is produced by the transformation of Will-to-Power into Numen, the sensual machine is produced by the transformation of Numen into Voluptas, and the masochistic machines are produced by the transformation of Voluptas back into Will-to-Power. The masochistic machines produce appropriations-ingestions of energy, the lack-machine produces recordings of energy, and the sensual machine produces a reservoir of energy for the masochistic machines. The Will-to-Power is the lust to possess the object of desire, and the failure to possess the object of desire results in the conversion of the Will-to-Power into Numen and thus the inscription of memories, and as the memories of the failure to possess the object of desire accumulate, quantities of tension increase exponentially, resulting in the conversion of Numen into Voluptas, which is essentially both surplus energy, surplus quantities of tension, and the surplus of the feeling of the failure to possess the object of desire. The feeling of the failure to possess the object of desire in turn feeds, stimulates, and inflames the lust to possess the object of desire, which is the process whereby Voluptas is reconverted into Will-to-Power.

The Intelligence of the Unconscious Mind

All subjectivity and behaviour are active and dynamic. Intelligence is a quality of active subjectivity and behaviour. Organisms utilize intelligence not only to adapt to their environment, but also to adapt their environment to themselves, modifying their environment in order to gratify their own drives. Each and every organism lives in a variable, competitive, and unpredictable environment that requires forms of behaviour that can overcome obstacles and gain victory in conflicts, forms of behaviour which are flexible enough to be able to deal with new obstacles and conflicts as they arise in an unpredictable environment. Those organisms best able to master their environment are those most likely to succeed in nature's power struggles.

Warwick writes, "When we compare the important aspects of intelligence, it is those which allow one species to dominate and exert power over other species that are of prime importance" (2001, p. 9). The variability, competitiveness, and unpredictability of the environment is largely constituted by the variability, competitiveness, and unpredictability of other organisms, the alterity of the other. All organisms are engaged in power struggles that result from each of their drives to possess their object of desire. Because the environment is constituted by conflicts, the power dynamics of intelligence are the most pertinent to the life of the organism, which consists of power struggles. Indeed, it is in relation to the dynamics and energetics of conflicts that the organism's cognition and behaviour develop, and it is in relation to the dynamics and energetics of conflicts that the organism integrates sensory data, forms associative memories, performs calculations, and makes decisions.

The property of intelligence has been so widely recognized by biologists as ubiquitous in living organisms throughout each of the various kingdoms of life that it would be absurd to not ascribe the property of intelligence to the unconscious mind, especially given that the vast majority of organisms are considered to be wholly unconscious by many biologists. Hellingwerf et al. (1995) demonstrate that the connections between proteins in bacteria enabled by phosphorylation is analogous to the connections between the dendrites of neurons in the brains of higher animals. Thus, Hellingwerf et al. (1995) describe the brain-like network of protein phosphorylation in bacteria as a "phosphoneural network."

According to Trewavas (2006, p. 6), the properties of these phosphoneural networks include "signal amplification, associative responses (cross talk) and memory effects." More research has indicated that bacteria are capable of learning (Hoffer et al. 2001; Trewavas 2006, p. 6) and that phosphoneural networks, which are relatively simple computational networks, process information and make informed decisions for bacterial cells (Bijlsma and Groisman 2003), meaning that bacterial cells posses "a rudimentary form of intelligence" (Trewavas 2006, p. 6). A bacterial cell is capable of forming associative memories and of formulating predictions of future events, which are two fundamental attributes of human intelligence (Trewavas 2006, p. 6; Hellingwerf 2005; La Cerra and Bingham 1998). Other fundamental attributes of human intelligence present in bacterial cells are sensory integration, memory, decision making, and the control of behaviour (Allmann 1999; Trewavas 2006, p. 6). La Cerra (2003) concludes that bacteria, the "simplest of animals," possess a "prototypical centralized intelligence system that has the same essential design characteristics and problem-solving logic as is evident in all animal intelligence systems, including humans" (as quoted in Trewavas 2006, p. 6). In other words, the phosphoneural network of a bacterial cell is analogous to the brain and the bacterial cell performs the same kind of intelligent behaviour that we typically attribute to more complex organisms that possess a brain, such as humans. Single-celled amoebas also evince intelligent behaviour, and have been observed to use several strategic methods in order to change its position, deliberately hunt motile infusoria for food, or to evade being impaled (Trewavas 2006, pp. 6-7; Grasse 1977). The slime mould *Physarum* can navigate mazes in order to achieve goals; Trewavas (2006, p. 7) writes that the "slime mould *Physarum* has been presented with a maze of differing lengths with food at the end and always chose the shortest path, indicating an ability to optimize food gain whilst minimizing economy of effort (Nakagaki et al. 2000). The authors of this paper state "this remarkable process of cellular computation implies that cellular materials can show a primitive intelligence."" The slime mould *Physarum*'s ability to navigate labyrinths in order to optimally achieve personal goals suggests that it too possesses a brain-like, prototypical centralized intelligence system with the same design characteristics and problem-solving logic as the intelligence systems of higher animals, including humans. A large and ever-increasing body of evidence also concludes that plants possess intelligence and brain-like information processing systems (cf. *Communication in Plants: Neuronal Aspects of Plant Life*, edited by Baluška, Mancuso, and Volkmann, 2006). In the light of this overwhelming evidence regarding the ubiquity of intelligence in living organisms, we must conclude that intelligence is an essential property of the unconscious mind. If such simple organisms as bacteria and slime moulds possess intelligence, and if even sessile organisms such as plants possess intelligence, then it must be the case that the unconscious mind possesses intelligence, since the activities of the unconscious mind are of the same essential nature as all these organisms (viz. information processing, sensory integration, forming memories, forming associative memories, making decisions, controlling behaviour, problem-solving, predictive modelling, optimizing achievement of goals and minimizing economy of effort). The unconscious mind is an information processing system of such complexity, integration, adaptive competence, and agency that it is scientifically fruitful to regard it as intelligent.

What Trewavas (2006, p. 3) writes of plant intelligence in the following passage applies, mutatis mutandis, to the intelligence of the unconscious mind in general: "In seeking to understand the biological origins of human intelligence, Stenhouse (1974) described intelligence as adaptively variable behaviour during the lifetime of the individual in an attempt to discriminate intelligent behaviour from autonomic, that is unvarying, responses. Given the plethora of signals that plants integrate into a response, autonomic responses do not occur. Signal perception is instead ranked according to assessments of strength and exposure. But autonomic responses can be rejected; the numbers of different environments that any wild plant experiences must be almost infinite in number." For much of the twentieth century, human intelligence has been considered either as only a function of consciousness or as a pure physiological function independent of any subjectivity whatsoever. The latter conclusion is absurd, whereas the former conclusion is extremely limited in its scope of investigation. A large body of evidence exists which supports *dual attitude theory*, the theory that *implicit attitudes* within the human organism make decisions for that organism, overriding the *explicit attitude* of that organism (cf. Wilson et al. 2000). Although Freud is rarely if at all mentioned in much of the research literature on dual attitude theory, the fact that dual attitude theory supports some of the most fundamental propositions of Freud's psychoanalysis is abundantly clear (viz. the existence of an unconscious mind, the importance of the unconscious mind in the decision-making process, the capacity of the unconscious mind to actively make decisions for the organism independently of consciousness, the capacity of consciousness to unknowingly disguise the true, unconscious attitude of the psyche). As we recount in *The Science of Self-Actualization*, one of Nietzsche's main discoveries was that the body itself thinks, feels, and wills, and we discovered that the unconscious mind and the body are one and the same entity, and it is to this concept of the body that we gave the name *body without organs*, borrowing a term from Antonin Artaud, not without justification. In other words, the body is an implicit cognitive system. The cognitive processes of the body constitute the implicit attitude of the organism. Psychoanalysis is the biology of the mind and the psychology of the body. We identify the explicit attitude as the system Cs and the implicit attitude as the system Ucs, and the fact that implicit attitudes make decisions for the organism, overriding the explicit attitude, means that the system Ucs makes decisions for the organism, bypassing the system Cs. The adaptively variable behaviour over the course of the lifetime of the individual, i.e. the individual's intelligence, is largely determined by the individual's implicit attitude, i.e. the individual's unconscious mind. In other words, the unconscious is an intelligent system. Our metapsychology differs from Freud in that we recognize perception as a function of the unconscious mind, and not of consciousness, hence we speak of the system Pcpt-Ucs. Given the plethora of signals that the system Pcpt-Ucs integrates into a response, autonomic responses by the system Pcpt-Ucs do not occur. The system Pcpt-Ucs interprets the psychosemiotic flows and signalectic flows it appropriates and consumes according to assessments of the quantity of intensity of the flow and the length of exposure to the flow, as well as according to the qualitative category of whether or not the flow reproduces the conditions of production of the system Ucs. However, the hypothesis that the unconscious mind performs autonomic, that is unvarying, responses can be rejected, because the plethora of different environments that any human being, and with them their unconscious mind, experiences *in natura* is approximately infinite in number.

Trewavas writes, "Plants and animals are not passive objects in the face of environmental disturbance…They react and positively fashion themselves according to the information (signals) they received" (2006, p. 2). This applies, mutatis mutandis, to the system

Pcpt-Ucs. In fact, plants, animals, and all other organisms are primarily metapsychological systems, and it is their system Pcpt-Ucs which primarily mediates their perception of and interaction with the environment. The system Pcpt-Ucs is not a passive object at the mercy of the forces of the environment. The system Pcpt-Ucs reacts and positively fashions itself according to the psychosemiotic flows and signalectic flows it appropriates, consumes, and interprets. The system Pcpt-Ucs is an active and intelligent system that actively and selectively gathers information (signals) from the environment and then processes that information and integrates it with internal information in order to positively construct itself and positively construct a response that reproduces the conditions of its mode of production. Only complex computation by the system Pcpt-Ucs can determine the optimal martial response in a given power-struggle of nature.

The psyche consists of organized structures, and vital properties coincide with the connections among the machinic constituents of which it is composed. Numerous machinic connections integrate into a more organized structure that we recognize as organic. In previous chapters, we discussed the structures of the psyche in terms of an economic model based largely on the work of Deleuze and Guattari's *Anti-Oedipus* and in terms of a dynamic model based largely on Freud, Stanislavski, Nietzsche, Lacan, and Leopardi. In this chapter, we outline a topographical model of the psyche, based largely on plant neurobiology. That is to say, we recognize certain structural analogies between the physiological structure of plants as outlined by plant neurobiologists (particularly in the volume *Communication in Plants: Neuronal Aspects of Plant Life*, mentioned above) and the metapsychological structure of the psyche as suggested by our findings, thus we use the physiological structure of the plant as a model for understanding psychological processes. We propose our topographical model of the psyche to differentiate our psychoanalytic theories from those of Freud, particularly from the topographical model he outlines in *The Ego and the Id*, which fails to account for the existence, primacy, and active nature of the unconscious perceptual system.

Desiring-machines are intelligent machines which function analogously to plants. The two main modules of the desiring-machine, the system Pcpt-Ucs and the system Mnem-Ucs, function together as an intelligent system. The activity of the system Pcpt-Ucs is inseparable from and dependent upon the activity of the system

Mnem-Ucs. However, for the sake of brevity we refer to the system Pcpt-Ucs as an intelligent system since it is the active agency of the desiring-machine; but we ask the reader to keep in mind the fact that the system Pcpt-Ucs always functions together with the system Mnem-Ucs, and that the system Cs is the residuum of desiring-production and the reservoir of energy for desiring-machines. The system Pcpt-Ucs of the totality of the psyche is the combined functioning of the unit-systems Pcpt-Ucs of the desiring-machines that constitute the psyche. Likewise, the system Mnem-Ucs of the totality of the psyche is the combined functioning of the unit-systems Mnem-Ucs of the desiring-machines that constitute the psyche. The desiring-machines constitutive of the system Pcpt-Ucs of the psyche are analogous to the root-apices, or root-brains, of the plant. Each plant has a multiplicity of root-apices that function as a multiplicity of brains for the plant. Each root apex is a brain, a command centre, and there is a multiplicity of such command centres in the physiology of the plant. This multiplicity of centres is a paradox, since it implies that there is no single, overarching centre, i.e. that there is no centre. However, the plant is nonetheless an intelligent organism, which means that the intelligence of the plant is decentralized, its intelligence system is a decentralized intelligence system, fragment into modules or unit-systems which are intelligent systems unto themselves (the multiplicity of root-brains). The psyche generally, in each and every case, is a decentralized intelligence system, consisting of a multiplicity of unit-systems of intelligence, the desiring-machines. Each desiring-machine is a brain, and the unconscious consists of a multiplicity of brains. Because its root-apices are the brains of the plant, the roots are the plant's anterior pole (its front) and its shoots are its posterior pole (its back). Likewise, the system Pcpt-Ucs is the anterior pole of the psyche and the system Cs is the posterior pole of the psyche.

Consciousness is visible, but the unconscious is invisible. The categories of space and movement (in space), as essential as they are as qualities of consciousness, do not apply to the unconscious, since the unconscious and the environment both consist of psychic forces, i.e. of subjectivities, and not objects which would constitute space. As Descartes correctly observes in his *Meditations*, spatiality is not an essential quality of subjectivity, meaning that subjectivity is essentially non-spatial. In our metapsychology, space is part of the hallucination which constitutes consciousness. Why then do we employ the metaphor of space in constructing our topographical model of the unconscious? And how do we account for movement without resorting to the concept of space? We answer that metaphors are indispensable to facilitate understanding, especially such a fundamental metaphor as that of space. Moreover, our topographical model of the plant conveys qualities of the unconscious such as intelligence and decentralization which we would otherwise be at a loss to so concisely convey. As for the question of movement in space, we can simply extend our metaphor of the plant and use plant movement as the metapsychological structure of all movement, including animal movement. A metapsychology of movement must attempt to explain the movement of unconscious subjectivities in a milieu consisting solely of subjectivities, and thus without the concept of space.

The unconscious experiences time differently than consciousness. For the unconscious, time moves much slower, each moment seemingly lasting an eternity, akin to the conscious experience of time during a psychedelic trip on LSD or psilocybin mushrooms. What to consciousness seems like an instantaneous action occurs, for the unconscious, over a vast stretch of time. Although time for consciousness and the unconscious may be measured with the same clock, the subjective experience of time is significantly different in each case; what for consciousness feels like one minute may, for the unconscious, feel like days, months, years, or even centuries or millennia. Freud also writes that the unconscious does not know time as such, but only a seeming eternity, and it is on the basis of Freud's conclusion in conjunction with reports on the psychedelic experience and the insight it offers us into the cognitive processes of the unconscious that we argue that the unconscious experiences a seeming eternity while consciousness experiences time. It is on the basis of the torturously slow pace of time in the subjective experience of the unconscious that we propose that all movement, even what appears to consciousness to be almost imperceptibly rapid and instinctive movement, happens a longer subjective timescale for the unconscious, akin to the pace of the growth of plant roots, and the predictive modelling performed by the unconscious encompasses such seemingly rapid actions as well as timescales of years or even decades in the life of the individual.

We conclude that the most parsimonious metapsychological explanation of movement must regard movement in terms of the growth of metapsychological structures, or metapsychological systems, which is analogous to plant movement, since the movement of plants is described by biologists precisely in terms of the growth of plant structures, namely the growth of its root apices. The movement of the system Ucs consists of the growth of metapsychological structures at the cost of the expenditure of energy, employs predictive modelling, and functions in the service of optimal domination. The system Pcpt-Ucs, the anterior pole of the psyche, is responsible for the organism's forward movement. The metapsychological root apices of the system Pcpt-Ucs drive an exploratory mode of metapsychological root growth in which the search is for the conditions of the mode of production, in order to feed the whole body without organs. Growing metapsychological root apices screen numerous environmental parameters, process this semiological data, and change psychological growth direction accordingly. Thus, metapsychological root apices behave both like plant root apices and, fittingly enough, like more active animals, performing highly efficient exploratory movements in their search for psychosemiotic resources.

Plant roots navigate the labyrinth of soil, which consists not only of soil and minerals, but also of the roots of other plants and even other organisms, some of which pose a threat. Likewise, the system Pcpt-Ucs is immersed in a medium of psychic forces, or psychosemiotic fluid, which it navigates, and the systems Pcpt-Ucs of other organisms are also immersed in this medium. There is a phenotypic plasticity of the system Ucs, meaning that the system Ucs has the ability to change the metapsychological structures which constitute it, and it is by means of the phenotypic plasticity of the system Ucs that the metapsychological root-apices of desiring-machines selectively grow, analogous to the root-apices of plants, in order to maximize the acquisition of resources and minimize damage to itself. The system Pcpt-Ucs actively forages for psychosemiotic resources, its psychosemiotic alimentation, by changing its metapsychological architecture and political physiology (its metapsychological phenotype). When patches of rich psychosemiotic resources are located by the system Pcpt-Uc and occupation of its psychosemiotic resource receptors reaches critical levels, the system Pcpt-Ucs makes decisions to initiate proliferation, or growth, of its metapsychological structures, thus greatly increasing its metapsychological surface area for the absorption of psychosemiotic flows. Decisions by desiring-machines are thus made continually as the system Pcpt-Ucs selectively grows, placing metapsychological structures analogous to root-apices in optimal positions according to the quantity of perceived psychosemiotic resources. Moreover, individual bodies without organs compete rigorously with each other for psychosemiotic resources and their decisions are designed to increase their own domination at the expense of others.

One of Nietzsche's greatest discoveries is that perception is essentially semiotic, since perception is essentially the interpretation of signs. To paraphrase Nietzsche, "There is no event in itself, there are only interpretations, and there is no "correct" interpretation" (cf. Nietzsche, WLN, N1, 115). Nietzsche's discovery is also confirmed by Proust, who also concludes that all perception to be semiotic in nature, and expands upon this conclusion, analysing each being as an emitter of signs. Deleuze, explicating Proust's *In Search of Lost Time*, writes, "To learn is first of all to consider a substance, an object, a being as if it emitted signs to be deciphered, interpreted" (1964/1972, p. 4). The work of Nietzsche and Proust is also supported by the work of Jacques Derrida, especially his treatise on semiology, *Of Grammatology*, in which Derrida also concludes that everything is semiotic, since he concludes that the sign is originary. The scientific discoveries of Nietzsche, Proust, and Derrida in the field of semiology, although they are not credited for them, are also supported by a large body of scientific evidence accumulated by the scientific discipline of *biosemiotics*, which has as its foundation the conclusion that all biological processes are in essence semiological processes (cf. *Introduction to Biosemiotics: The New Biological Synthesis*, edited by Marcello Barbieri, 2007). On this basis, we describe Nietzsche, Proust, and Derrida as the uncredited pioneers of biosemiotics. Furthermore, the scientific work of Freud reveals that all processes consist, in terms of their psychology, of the dynamics, energetics, and economics of the libido. In biosemiotics terms, flows of libido are always already semiotic flows. Therefore, we use the term *psychosemiotic* to denote the libido (viz. psychosemiotic flows are libidinal flows or flows of libido). As we have stated earlier, all material flows are in actuality psychosemiotic flows. Thus, all perception has the same structure as alimentation because both perception and alimentation consist of the appropriation, consumption, and digestion, or interpretation, of psychosemiotic flows; hence why we describe the perceptual activity of desiring-machines as the appropriation-consumption of psychosemiotic flows. Previously, in *The Science of Self-Actualization* (Kasem 2018, p. 191), we concluded, "The psychic forces which constitute the external world are all so many sources of forces-qualia, all so many emitters of signs. A source of forces-qualia is an emitter of signs; this source is a psychic force, a multiplicity of psychic forces, and these signs are psychic forces. In other words, a source of psychic forces is an emitter of psychic forces." Forces, qualia, and signs are in fact the same entity described by different names which highlight its different aspects; we here use the term *psychosemiotic flows* in an attempt to encompass all these different aspects of force with a single name. When Proust writes of all beings as emitters of signs, we may say, in order to account for the discoveries of both biosemiotics and psychoanalysis, that all beings are systems of psychosemiotic flows and of interruptions of psychosemiotic flows, i.e. desiring-machines. That a being is an emitter of signs, a source of forces-qualia, and an emitter of psychic forces means that a being is a source and emitter of libido, or psychosemiotic flows, and a source and emitter of psychosemiotic flows is a system of psychosemiotic flows, more specifically it is a system of flows of libido and interruption of flows of libido, which means that it is a desiring-machine. The forces which constitute beings are all active forces, thus the perceptual system of the system Ucs is always an active system, never a passive one. Therefore, we must amend Proust's description of perception as the reception of emissions of signs. We emphasize that the perceptual system is a system of active forces, meaning that it is spontaneous and self-directing system. To clarify, in our model of perception, the subject is not a passive receiver of the signs emitted by other organisms, but rather, the subject is an active forager for the signs emitted by other organisms.

Moreover, we reject the concept of "fitness" as it is commonly employed because it is a teleological concept, whereas nature and history are non-teleological and aleatoric. To clarify, we accept that evolution, descent with modification, occurs, but we reject that the mechanism by which it occurs is "natural selection," because "natural selection" is a teleological concept, whereas evolution is non-teleological. Therefore, the measurement of "fitness," which purports to measure "natural selection" (as in "survival of the fittest") by measuring an individual's capacity to reproduce, is a false, useless, and superfluous concept. As we argued in *The Science of Self-Actualization*, "fitness" is a pure concept that cannot be deduced strictly from physiological data (Kasem 2018, pp. 141-160). In other words, "fitness" is an intellectual model superimposed upon physiological data. As such, it is not only the case that "fitness" is a social construct, but it is also the case that the concept of "fitness" is open to the criticisms of reason, in order that more rational concepts can be employed to understand evolution. We cite the arguments of Friedrich Nietzsche that life is characterized by the struggle for power, not by the "struggle for existence," that the principle of evolution is the chance elimination, or random elimination, of individuals and species regardless of their qualities (e.g. in mass extinction events), and that species do not evolve towards an ideal of perfection (cf. TI, "Skirmishes of an Untimely Man," 14; Kasem 2018, pp. 141-160). The concept of "fitness" is just such an ideal of perfection. If fitness existed, then each generation would optimize its own fitness, meaning that each subsequent generation would increase the fitness of the species, as if the species were gradually evolving towards the optimum degree of fitness, which would be the final and perfect state of fitness. Obviously, nature does not work in such a fashion, which is why we reject the concepts of fitness and natural selection. Evolution is non-teleological, meaning that it does *not* tend towards a state of "perfection." We propose Nietzsche's genealogical model of history, which analyses history in terms of power struggles and accounts for change in terms of the increased degree of domination of a force, to be applicable to evolution. Genealogy is the mechanism of evolution. Because nature consists of power struggles, we propose that it is more scientifically fruitful to understand the cognition and behaviour of organisms in terms of power dynamics, that is to say, in terms of their degree of domination, bearing in mind that power struggles emerge from the conflicting motivations of organisms and that different forces within an organism may at different times be the dominant force of that organism. An organism strives primarily to possess its object of desire and secondarily to reproduce its conditions of production (i.e. its mode of crystallization). Although an organism can never possess its object of desire, since its object of desire is always a fantasy, an organism can and does reproduce its conditions of production. Therefore, an organism's degree of domination must be measured in terms of its success or failure to reproduce its conditions of production. Each organism is a form of domination, or will to power, insofar as it strives to reproduce its conditions of production. Furthermore, when an organism's mode of production is altered, its form of domination is likewise altered, which means that there are ruptures in the evolution of a species, such that the species does not tend towards a single perfect ideal of domination, but the evolution of a species consists of the transformation of forms of domination (modification with descent = transformation of forms of domination = transformations of modes of production), wherein each successive form of domination has conditions of production different from, or even antithetical to, the last.

Predictive modelling of behavioural outcomes in the service of increased domination is an important aspect of intelligent behaviour. Virtually all decisions made by an organism are directed towards a future goal of optimal domination, given the parameters of the form of domination which characterizes the species and the form of domination which characterizes the singularity, or individuality, of the organism in question. We reiterate that these decisions are made by the system Ucs of the organism. The system Ucs predicts future changes in the availability of psychosemiotic resources. The system Pcpt-Ucs is self-sensing and territorial, just like plant roots; the territorialisation of the system Ucs and its form of domination determines the behaviour of the organism. The metapsychological root apices of the system Pcpt-Ucs growing along gradients of psychosemiotic flows model a future that will subsequently increase psychosemiotic resource acquisition if continued. Even when psychosemiotic resource receptors are finally triggered and proliferation of metapsychological structures is initiated, predictive modelling is fully in effect because new metapsychological structures only become psychosemiotic sources when nearly fully constructed. Just as with plant roots, both negative and positive feedback controls operate to flesh out predictive models formed by the system Ucs (cf. Trewavas 2006, p. 10).

We agree with Deleuze and Guattari (1972/1977, p. 108) when they write, "The organized body is the object of reproduction by generation; it is not its subject. The sole subject of reproduction is the unconscious itself, which holds to the circular form of production. Sexuality is not a means in the service of generation; rather, the generation of bodies is in the service of sexuality as an autoproduction of the unconscious." There is no "reproductive urge" or "procreative urge" in itself. Rather, sexual reproduction is a function of the reproduction of the conditions of production. In other words, sexual desire (sexuality) is not a function of sexual reproduction (generation), sexual reproduction (generation) is a function of sexual desire (sexuality). We define sexual desire as the mode of production of the unconscious, which is the mode of production of fantasy or mode of crystallization. The "reproductive urge" of each desiring-machine is its ideological apparatus, its urge to reproduce its conditions of production, and this is what results in the generation of bodies. Therefore, an organism's capacity for sexual reproduction is a function of its capacity to reproduce its conditions of production. In other words, an organism's capacity for sexual reproduction is a function of its form of domination or degree of domination. This applies, mutatis mutandis, to asexual reproduction, which we maintain is a function of sexual desire insofar as it is a function of the libidinal economy of drives. Therefore, although the system Pcpt-Ucs of each desiring machine functions like a plant root, the totality of the ideological apparatus of a desiring-machine functions like a flower, since it is in effect a reproductive system, reproducing its conditions of production, the generation of bodies being the natural result of this system. In fact, insofar as the system Pcpt-Ucs acquires psychosemiotic resources in order to reproduce the conditions of a desiring-machine's mode of production, it is a module of the ideological apparatus of a desiring-machine, meaning that it is a module of the reproductive system of a desiring-machine. Each form of domination is a form of reproduction. Here, our topographical model departs from the description of plants, since in plants the posterior pole is the roots and the anterior pole is the shoots with their leaves and flowers, whereas in our topographical model of the psyche the entire unconscious is the anterior pole and functions simultaneously as the roots and the flowers of the psyche, while consciousness is the posterior pole and functions as the reservoir of the psyche.

The Flowers of the Body without Organs

The signs emitted by the body without organs are its flowers; these emissions constitute the surface of the body without organs. The surfaces of bodies without organs are primarily what constitute perception-images, and part of these movement-images is what comes to consciousness. Hence the separation of the visible and the invisible, between the surface of bodies and the subjectivity of bodies. The genesis of surfaces makes possible the deceptions that constitute our lived experience, especially our social life and our love life. We discovered earlier that each desiring-machine is both a flow-ingesting machine and a flow-producing machine. Surfaces are psychosemiotic flows emitted by desiring-machines from so many pores, as it were, just as a scent is emitted.

We describe the surface of the body without organs as its *style*, after Derrida's concept of style, which he develops in *Spurs: Nietzsche's Styles*. Derrida writes, "In the question of style there is always the weight or *examen* [the examination, or, the tongue of a balance] of some pointed object. At times this object might be only a quill or a stylus. But it could just as easily be a stiletto, or even a rapier. Such objects might be used in a vicious attack against what philosophy appeals to in the name of matter or matrix, an attack whose thrust could not but leave its mark, could not but leave its mark, could not but inscribe there some imprint or form. But they might also be used as protection against the threat of such an attack, in order to keep it at a distance, to repel it—as one bends or recoils before its force, in flight, derrière des voiles (behind its sails and veils)" (1979, p. 37). Style is surface, surface is style. Style impresses or inscribes signs, thus it is a stylus, a metapsychological writing instrument that writes upon the mystic writing pad of the unconscious. Style is an ornament, because it is surface and therefore superficial, but because it ornaments drives to violence it is an ornament of violence. Style is a weapon, an instrument of violence and a force of violence which operates by means of attacks, counterattacks, defences, and feints. Style is stylus, ornament, and weapon. Style, because it is appearance and not essence, deceives. Style is deception. Style is produced by a drive, but it expresses a drive only in that it is used by that drive as a means to an end, that is to say, style obscures, style disguises the drive which produces it. Style is a mask. The genesis of style is the genesis of surfaces that make possible the masquerade that is our lived experience. A flower is a system of deception and a system of style. A flower is a weapon. Nature has a multiplicity of styles. The pointed object whose weight bears upon the question of style is always both a sword and a pen simultaneously. A style is always both a sword and a pen simultaneously. A style is a system of violence and a system of inscription. Writing is violence, violence is writing. The writing of bodies upon each other is primarily the psychic writing, or metapsychological writing, of surfaces. Style is communication. Style is always suited to the specific type of body, and even the individual body, with whom it communicates. Because conflict is originary, all relations are power relations and relations of violence, meaning that communication is always an act of violence. From a different line of argument we arrive at the same conclusion: communication is always an act of violence because communication is always an act of deception. A style is always an action, an action which is invariably an act of war. The eternal conflict and violence of the multiplicity of forces of existence is always already the eternal conflict and violence of the multiplicity of styles, which are the surfaces of the forces of existence. The swords of the forces of existence eternally deceive, attack, defend. Les voiles des styles sont violence, les voiles de violence sont styles, les styles des voiles sont violence, les styles de violence sont les voiles, la violence des voiles sont les styles.

Derrida writes that style is an *éperon*, or *spur*: "Thus the style would seem to advance in the manner of a *spur* of sorts (*éperon*). Like the *prow*, for example, of a sailing vessel, its *rostrum*, the projection of the ship which surges ahead to meet the sea's attack and cleave its hostile surface. Or yet again, and still in nautical terminology, the style might be compared to that rocky point, also called an *éperon*, on which the waves break at the harbor's entrance" (ibid, p. 39). Derrida writes that the spur of style, the style-spur, is also, like the German *Spur*, a "trace, wake, indication, mark," i.e. a sign (ibid, p. 41). A style is a sign, or rather, a style is a system of signs, hence why the genesis of surfaces is the emission of signs. Derrida's concept of the *éperon*, or *spur*, combines the diverse meanings of different but related words: the spur which goads, as on a pair of riding boots; the nautical éperon, the prow of a sailing vessel; the other nautical éperon, the rocky point on which the waves break at the harbour's entrance; spurning, disdaining, rebuffing, rejecting scornfully (cf. ibid, pp. 39-41); and the German Spur, the trace, wake, indication, mark, or sign; Derrida's éperon or spur contains all these diverse meanings simultaneously, combining them. For Derrida, the spur is an essential quality of style: "The style-spur, the spurring style, is a long object, an oblong object, a word, which perforates even as it parries. It is the oblong-foliated point (a spur or a spar) which derives its apotropaic power from the taut, resistant tissues, webs, voiles (sails and veils) which are erected, furled and unfurled around it" (ibid, p. 41). A style is a sign, meaning in Derrida's terminology that a style is a system of difference and mediation, difference and deferment. Style parries and defends, meaning that style defers. Style deceives, and the deception of style is another form of deferment. When style parries and defends, it defers the domination of the other, in the service of the increased domination of the self. When style deceives, it defers the truth of the self, also in the service of the increased domination of the self. Therefore, in a two-fold sense, encompassing both defence and deception, style is a form of deferment, meaning that style is a form of mediation. The mediation of style is a function of the form of domination which produces style. Mediation is violence, violence is mediation. Derrida himself suggests the fundamental identity of mediation and violence in *Of Grammatology*, particularly in his critique of Lévi-Strauss, when he discovers that deception is originary, and as a consequence of this, he also discovers that violence is originary; furthermore, throughout *Of Grammatology* he argues that mediation, difference, and writing are originary, which suggests a fundamental similarity, if not equivalence, between mediation, difference, writing, and violence. The surface of the body is always the surface of violence and the violence of surface, since its functions are to deceive, attack, and defend. The surface of the body perforates even as it parries, it is a spurring, sparring style, a spar-spur, a style-sword; or rather, a multiplicity of style-swords. The surface of the body is a system of difference, and it is its difference, its difference from the essence or subjectivity of the body as well as its difference from other surfaces, that makes possible its efficacy as a system of deception. The surface of the body differs not only from the truth of the body, but it also differs from other surfaces.

Appearance deceives and appearance seduces. Appearance is deception and appearance is seduction. The surface of the body is a system of seduction. Seduction is the art of promising pleasure, but pleasure by its very nature is something that can never be experienced. Seduction is deception. The body emits a seductive surface in the service of the increased domination of its form of domination. Such is the power of seduction and the seduction of power. The surface of the body is simultaneously both a spur which goads and a spur which spurns. Style is a whip. The surface of the body is, to borrow Derrida's phrase, a *stylate spur* (*éperon style*), it inscribes its signs upon the perceptual apparatuses of other bodies, and this inscription is performed by means of the inscription of excitations and, inextricable from and coextensive with those positive quantities of excitations, negative quantities of potentialities for pleasure. The genesis of the body's surface is the fabrication of taut, resistant tissues, webs, veils, and sails which are erected, furled, and unfurled in the negative space of difference. These fabricated taut, resistant tissues, webs, veils, and sails function as systems of inscription, deception, seduction, attack, and defence. These surfaces are flowers and faces, flesh and figures, glances and gestures, sounds and scents, words and meanings, but most of all these surfaces, in all their various forms, are masks. The genesis of surfaces is the writing of masks.

The Oedipus Complex and Primal Repression

In neurosis, the Oedipus complex and primal repression constitute the implicit attitude of the subject, whereas the repressive drive constitutes the explicit attitude. Freud writes that *"the essence of repression lies simply in the function of rejecting and keeping something out of consciousness*…Now, we have reason for assuming *a primal repression,* a first phase of repression, which consists in a denial of entry into consciousness to the mental (ideational) presentation of the instinct" (1915, p. 86). The "mental presentation" or "ideational presentation" of the drive refers to the fantasy which serves as the aim of the drive. In the primal repression of early childhood, it is the Oedipal fantasy of the sex drive which is repressed, denied entry into consciousness. The Oedipus complex is repressed, but it is never truly resolved, since it remains alive in the unconscious, continuing to exert an influence upon our motivations, desires, feelings, thoughts, and actions. But how does repression function? What does it mean to keep the mental content of a drive from coming into consciousness? We may begin to answer this question using the model of the psyche we have thus far constructed.

Consciousness is the surplus-value of excitations of an unconscious drive, and a drive acquires excitations via its system Pcpt-Ucs, which appropriates and consumes quantities of excitations from the environment in order to reproduce the conditions of existence of its mode of production, which is the fantasy which drives the drive. Repression occurs when a new drive is forged in the unconscious which becomes the dominant drive of the unconscious, thereby becoming the drive which appropriates and consumes excitations from the environment and produces the surplus value of excitations constitutive of consciousness. That is to say, repression occurs when a new drive is grafted upon the unconscious, this new drive being a parasite which feeds on the energy of the old drive, thereby dominating it. The mental presentation, or fantasy, of this new drive then becomes the dominant fantasy of the organism, the one which comes to consciousness, although the repressed drive and its fantasy are still alive and active in the unconscious. Repression causes a state of perpetual inner conflict between the repressing drive and the repressed drive, which is, to paraphrase Goethe, the state of having "two souls in one breast." Trauma is the mechanism by which a new drive is grafted upon the unconscious. Trauma inscribes a new memory, and with that new memory a new drive and a new fantasy, and it does so at the expense of an older memory which is supplanted, or repressed, and with that older memory, its corresponding drive and fantasy are also supplanted, or repressed. The specific type of trauma that represses the Oedipus complex is the imposition of the incest taboo, what Freud calls *castration anxiety*, which we shall explore later in greater detail.

In terms of the three machines of desiring-production, the procedure of desiring-production is performed primarily upon the lack-machine, the socius of fantasy, and thereby produces its effects upon the masochistic machines and upon consciousness, the sensual machine. The socius of fantasy not only inscribes memories, but also miraculates desiring-production, that is to say, it reproduces desiring-production, such that desiring-production emanates from it. Desiring-machines are extensions and instruments of the power of the socius of fantasy. If the fantasy-crystals of crystallization are unit-objectives, then the socius of fantasy is the super-objective, the overarching objective of desiring-production, the foundation of its mode of production, that from which the fantasy-crystals of crystallization are derived. Repression is the grafting of a new socius which arrogates all desiring-production to itself and inscribes new memories for desiring-production in relation to a new fantasy, thereby serving as the central and prototypical fantasy of a new mode of production, producing a new form of desiring-production and subsequently reproducing this new form of desiring-production as the defining form of desiring-production for the body without organs.

It is clear that in an ideal case there is only one socius, one dominant fantasy of the body without organs, which would mean the smooth and efficient functioning of desiring-machines. However, in the vast majority of human beings, there are at least two conflicting fantasies, two conflicting socius, within one body without organs: the repressed fantasy-socius and the repressing fantasy-socius (or repressive fantasy-socius). When repression occurs, the repressing socius is grafted upon the original socius of the organism, upon which it feeds like a parasite. The procedure of repression transforms the original socius of the organism into the repressed socius as such. The repressing socius is a special kind of parasitic organism, one which has effectively fused with its host organism, since the repressing socius becomes the dominant socius of the organism, such that the corresponding repressive drive of the repressing socius becomes the dominant drive of the organism and the organism identifies itself with this repressive drive. It is important to note that the repressive socius only exists as such in relation to the repressed socius and the process of repression, meaning that the organism can identify itself with the repressive drive only because the repressed socius and its corresponding repressed drive are still alive within the organism, albeit in their repressed form.

Freud writes that "repression demands a constant expenditure of energy, and if this were discontinued the success of the repression would be jeopardized, so that a fresh act of repression would be necessary. We may imagine that what is repressed exercises a continuous straining in the direction of consciousness, so that the balance has to be kept by means of a steady counter-pressure" (1915, p. 89). Repression, even primal repression, is not simply a singular event, but an ongoing process. The system Pcpt-Ucs of the repressive drive must constantly acquire psychosemiotic forces from the environment for itself in order to have enough energy to continue to repress the repressed drive. The repressed drive always threatens to acquire enough energy to overpower the repressive drive, a process which, if successful, would result in the repressed drive producing enough surplus value of excitations to produce a state of consciousness. A large portion of the repressed drive's energy is siphoned off by the repressive drive, that is to say, the spontaneous and natural sexual energy of the repressed organism funds the very process of repression itself. The repressive drive does not have its own desiring-machines so much as it hijacks the desiring-machines of the repressed drive. The repressive socius of fantasy re-inscribes the repressed desiring-machines belonging to the repressed socius of fantasy with the code for the repressive mode of production, thereby producing and reproducing the repressive mode of production, and the repressive socius must maintain this re-inscription process in order to maintain repression. The natural motivations of desiring-machines, which result in the inscription of memories charged with emotional values in relation to the repressed fantasy, thus also results in the inscription of memories charged with emotional values in relation to the repressive fantasy, and in this way the natural energy of desiring-machines is used against them, since the more ardent the desire of the desiring-machines, i.e. the higher their quantity of libido, the more active the repressive socius of fantasy and the greater the overcoding of desire performed by the repressive socius. Meanwhile, the repressed drive, unable to acquire psychosemiotic energy via the perceptual apparatus, starves and is weakened, but is kept alive by direct or substitute means, the repressed signifying-chain appropriating for itself, usually by means of association, signs from the repressive signifying-chain. Moreover, since the repressive drive relies on the repressed drive for energy, when the repressed drive is low on energy the repressive drive is also low on energy, and in such times repression is at its weakest and the repressed drive manages to gain energy for itself, thereby also giving life to the parasitic repressive drive and renewing the cycle of repression. Repression is thus maintained by means of positive and negative feedback controls.

The aim, demand, and fantasy of the repressed drive is incompatible with the aim, demand, and fantasy of the repressive drive, which results in the repressed drive being held back at a lower level of psychical development and apparently cut off from the possibility of reproducing its conditions of production and acquiring quasi-pleasures. However, the repressed drive does indeed succeed in reproducing its conditions of production via roundabout paths, thereby achieving quasi-pleasure by direct or substitute means. In fact, the repressed sexual drive does this relatively easily and it does so often, and it is only because it keeps itself alive in this manner that the repressive drive likewise keeps itself alive. However, when the repressed drive does achieve quasi-pleasure, as Freud writes, "that event, which would in other cases have been an opportunity for pleasure, is felt by the ego as unpleasure" (1961, p. 5). Freud writes all *neurotic unpleasure* is of this kind, "pleasure that cannot be felt as such" (ibid). The repressed drive achieves quasi-pleasure by acquiring signs-excitations that reproduce its conditions of production, but because its mode of production and consequently the conditions of its mode of production are antithetical to the repressive drive's mode of production and the conditions of the repressive drive's mode of production, the ideological apparatus of the repressive drive interprets the repressed drive's quasi-pleasure as unpleasure. Because the repressive drive produces the surplus value of excitations which constitutes the system Cs, the system Cs likewise feels as unpleasure what, deep within the unconscious of the organism, the repressed drive had felt as quasi-pleasure. This kind of unpleasure felt by the system Cs is neurotic unpleasure, and it is the result of the cultural hegemony of a state of repression, which is a neurotic state. Repression produces neurosis. The Oedipal drive is the core of the unconscious, the core of the body, and the core of the organism, but it is evident that after the grafting of the parasitic repressive drive, the Oedipal drive in its repressed form is diseased, and ramifies and grows in a diseased state, mostly cut off from the external world and thereby cut off from a healthy development, living in a constant state of imprisonment and starvation, and forced to satisfy itself by indirect means. Neurosis is the direct result of repression, which is the conflict between one mode of libidinal cathexis of objects and another, different mode of libidinal cathexis of objects, namely the conflict between the repressed mode of production and the repressing mode of production (and their corresponding fabrication and cathexes of objects of desire), which is also the conflict between the repressed ideological apparatus and the repressing ideological apparatus (and their corresponding fabrications and cathexes of ideological constructs, as well as their corresponding appropriation-consumptions and cathexes of psychosemiotic flows). In other words, neurosis is the direct result of the coexistence in one psyche of two antithetical systems of values, each of which evaluates pleasures and pains on a basis antithetical to the other.

Freud writes that the instinct-presentation of the repressed drive, meaning in our terminology the repressed drive and its repressed socius of fantasy, develop "in a more unchecked and luxuriant fashion" on account of their being repressed and thus being cut off from access to the perceptual apparatus; there, in the depths of the unconscious, they ramify "like a fungus, so to speak, in the dark" and take on "extreme forms of expression," which is the "result of an uninhibited development…in phantasy and of the damming-up consequent on lack of real satisfaction" (1915, p. 87). In other words, the repressed drive remains active, which means that the repressed mode of production and the repressed ideological apparatus remain active, the repressed mode of production producing derivatives of the primally repressed fantasy and the ideological apparatus producing signs which reproduce the conditions of existence of the repressed mode of production. The repressed drive, a rhizome, reproduces rhizomatically, by means of underground stems which send additional shoots in every direction, upward, downward, and laterally, thereby acquiring psychosemiotic resources from the signifying-chain of the repressive drive and producing derivatives of the primally repressed fantasy which the repressive drive, in turn, appropriates and consumes, making them part of the repressive signifying-chain. Freud writes that if these derivatives of the primally repressed fantasy are "sufficiently far removed from the repressed instinct-presentation, whether owing to the process of distortion or by reason of the number of intermediate associations, they have free access to consciousness" (ibid, p. 88). The derivatives of the primally repressed fantasy which are able to be incorporated or introjected into the repressive signifying-chain, due to their sufficient removal from the primally repressed fantasy either due to their distortion or due to the number of intermediate associations separating them from the primally repressed fantasy, become conscious when they are included in the portion of the repressive signifying-chain which becomes the surplus value of the repressive desiring-production of the repressive drive. This kind of derivative of the primally repressed fantasy is a *neurotic derivative* or *neurotic symptom*. Neurotic derivatives are signs which pass the censorship of the repressive ideological apparatus of the unconscious. Neurotic derivatives are neurotic because they lack the innocence, directness, and naturalness of the derivatives, meaning both the objects of desires and ideological constructs, produced prior to the primal repression. Neurotic derivatives are distorted, roundabout means of satisfying the repressed drive, the satisfaction of which yields neurotic unpleasure for the subject. (We are speaking here, of course, of the pseudo-satisfaction of quasi-pleasure, and not of the true satisfaction of true pleasure). Neurotic derivatives sometimes succeed in satisfying the repressed drive by means of garnering new signs-excitations from the perceptual apparatus hijacked by the repressive signifying-chain or becoming associated with memory-traces constitutive of the repressive signifying-chain; these new signs-excitations, due to their association with the neurotic derivative, stimulate the activity of the repressed drive by means of all the intermediate associations between the neurotic drive and the primally repressed fantasy, and the repressed drive thereby appropriates, consumes, and introjects or incorporates these new signs-excitations into the repressed signifying-chain, thereby yielding quasi-pleasure for the repressed drive and neurotic unpleasure for the repressive drive.

Guilt is a form of neurotic unpleasure. In his book *On the Genealogy of Morals* Nietzsche conceived of guilt as the feeling of indebtedness and *bad conscience* as the feeling of self-torture. However, we do not conceive of guilt as the feeling of indebtedness, but in the more general sense which Nietzsche himself sometimes uses in other texts; that is to say, we conceive of guilt as equivalent to the feeling of self-torture, and thus we conceive of guilt as equivalent to bad conscience. To be more specific, "guilt" is a social construct used to label a feeling that results from the complex interactions of repressed and repressing drives. When the repressed drive produces a neurotic derivative and this neurotic derivative succeeds in acquiring a quasi-pleasure for the repressed drive, either from the perceptual apparatus or from the signifying-chain of the repressive drive, then the repressive drive experiences neurotic unpleasure, and when this neurotic unpleasure is produced in surplus amounts, it becomes a state of consciousness. "Guilt," considered as a concept, is a social construct and a falsification, which includes among its elements other falsifications such as the concept of "responsibility" and "free will" (which are absurd concepts considered from the scientific point of view, since all observable phenomena suggest that the world is deterministic and fatalistic, which consequently leaves absolutely no room for concepts such as "free will" and "responsibility"). However, this concept, "guilt," although it has no basis in reality, is used as a label for very real feelings, feelings which we have identified as the feeling of neurotic unpleasure. Because neurotic unpleasure is produced by repression, we may say that guilt is produced by repression. Repression, at bottom, is the imposition of the incest taboo, a phenomenon which Freud describes as castration anxiety; therefore, we can identify the mechanism which produces guilt as being, at bottom, the imposition of the incest taboo, which must be continually maintained and active in the unconscious in order for repression to likewise be continually maintained and active. Nietzsche describes bad conscience as arising from "fearful bulwarks with which the political organization protected itself against the old drives of freedom," and which "brought about that all those drives of wild, free, prowling man turned backward against man himself" (GM, II, 16). We have identified that fearful bulwark of political organization as repression, and we have identified the old drive of freedom as the Oedipal drive. In other words, the repressive drive is an inherently sociocultural and socio-political force, and this sociocultural and socio-political force produces the feeling of guilt. By means of repression the Oedipal drive is turned against itself; the Oedipal drive, cut off from the perceptual apparatus by the repressive drive, is no longer able to discharge itself into the environment, and thus discharges itself within the organism, which is felt as neurotic unpleasure by the repressive drive of the organism and consequently by consciousness. This means that the ramification of the repressed Oedipal drive within the unconscious is felt as neurotic unpleasure by the repressive drive and by consciousness; this ramification, or internal discharge, occurs only by means of the psychosemiotic resources acquired by neurotic derivatives, thus accounting for the neurotic unpleasure felt by the repressive drive. Guilt, which is the feeling of neurotic unpleasure, is thus caused not so much by a drive turning against itself, as Nietzsche believed, but by the conflict of two opposing drives within one psyche (the conflict of "two souls in one breast"). Nietzsche writes of bad conscience as the "will to self-maltreatment" (cf. Nietzsche, GM, II, 16-18), or in other words, the drive to self-torture. It is evident that guilt, in addition to being a feeling, can also be a drive unto itself, a veritable drive to self-torture (e.g. the self-flagellation of Christian monks; the spiritual self-flagellation of Christians generally). When guilt appears to be a drive to self-torture in the psyche, it is because it has been inscribed as such as an essential component of the repressive drive, such that this form of repression, which we may call *Christian repression* due to its major role in the pathology of Christianity, maintains itself as repression by means of producing neurotic unpleasures. In Christian repression, the repressive drive actively desires the feeling of neurotic unpleasure as an object of desire (viz. the fantasy of sin, especially original sin); the repressed Oedipal drive proliferates neurotic derivatives and thereby cunningly and indirectly acquires the psychosemiotic resources it needs to reproduce its mode of production, in however subterranean a fashion, and thus keep alive, and the repressive drive actively desires to keep alive the repressed drive in order to vampirically feed off its energy and reproduce the repressive mode of production, thereby keeping itself (the repressive drive) alive at the cost of actively desiring to feel more and more neurotic unpleasures. In other words, when guilt is a drive, it means that the production and reproduction of neurotic unpleasure is the part of the signifying-chain, the very code, of the repressive drive.

Freud writes that although primal repression is the primary form of repression, there is also a secondary form of repression, or second phase of repression, which follows from the first, and which "concerns mental derivatives of the repressed instinct-presentation, or such trains of thought as, originating elsewhere, have come into associative connection with it. On account of this association, these ideas experience the same fate as that which underwent primal repression" (1915, p. 86). This secondary repression, which Freud calls "repression proper," is also commonly called "denial." It is clearly evident that primal repression also subsequently entails the repression of the mental derivatives of the primally repressed fantasy, meaning both the repressed objects of desire manufactured by the repressed drive's mode of production and the repressed ideological constructs fabricated by the ideological apparatus of the repressed drive. It is important to note, however, that trains of thought originating elsewhere than in the psyche, i.e. trains of thought from the external world, if they are associated with the primally repressed fantasy or resonate with the primally repressed fantasy, are likewise repressed; this form of repression is the defence mechanism of denial. Denial appears to be the rejection of something in the external world; however, for a phenomenon to be denied, it must first be perceived, i.e. incorporated or introjected, by the system Pcpt-Ucs, which means that the denied phenomenon is still, strictly speaking, in the psyche. Freud writes that here the repressed drive is in a way just as responsible for the denial as the repressive drive, since the repressed drive exerts a force of *attraction* "upon everything with which it can establish a connection," thereby assimilating that which is rejected by the repressive drive (ibid, p. 87). We argue that this force of "attraction" is more accurately described in terms of the intelligence of the repressed drive, which because it is alive continues to actively forage for psychosemiotic resources, and appropriates and consumes those signs-excitations from the signifying-chain of the repressive drive which reproduce its (the repressed drive's) conditions of production. Moreover, we note that all phenomena from the external world apprehended by the psyche are of the nature of perceptions, since even "trains of thought" from the external world can only be known via the perception of one medium or another (e.g. language, cinema, music). Perceptions, after they have been introjected or incorporated by the perceptual apparatus and have become perceptions as such, are signs-excitations which are part of the signifying-chain of the drive which operates the perceptual apparatus. Thus, the defence mechanism of denial always concerns the denial of perceptions. When the repressed drive introjects or incorporates that which is denied by the repressive drive, the repressed drive experiences quasi-pleasure, and consequently the repressive drive and consciousness experience neurotic unpleasure. The denial of facts generally, when it is a sincere denial and not merely a hypocritical political tactic, is denial in the psychoanalytic sense (e.g. Climate change denial is hypocritical political tactic employed by the executives of fossil fuel companies and politicians who actually know climate change to be a real crisis, but for those who sincerely deny climate change, refusing to believe in its reality, climate change denial is a neurotic symptom with its roots in the Oedipus complex). Faced with a case of denial, the key question to ask is which aspect of the Oedipus complex, through its association with the denied sign or series of signs, is being denied. In this way, one can infer the nature of the illness from the symptom, and thereby develop a cure.

Nietzsche's concept of *ressentiment* refers to the feeling of resentment, which is the sustained, long-term, and pathological drive of revenge. Nietzsche writes that ressentiment is produced when subjects are "denied the true reaction, that of deeds, and compensate themselves with an imaginary revenge" (GM, I, 10). We recognize ressentiment as a universal psychological trait in humans, as universal as the Oedipus complex and primal repression. That is to say, we have concluded that ressentiment has its roots in the Oedipus complex of the child, more specifically in the homicidal sexual jealousy the child feels towards his father; the child wishes to exact revenge upon the father for the father's sexual possession of the mother, whom the child wants to exclusively possess, but the child, being physically far weaker and smaller than the father, is unable expel his patricidal urge by expending it with a deed. Subsequently, the child's jealous patricidal fantasy, along with its cause, his sexual desire for the mother, undergoes primal repression due to the imposition of castration anxiety. Primal repression denies the true reaction of the child's patricidal wish, that of deeds, and thereupon, as the repressed Oedipal drive ramifies in the unconscious, it continues producing patricidal fantasies as objects of desire, and thus his patricidal drive achieves quasi-satisfaction in the same way that his sexual desire for the mother achieves quasi-satisfaction, namely in a distorted form, through numerous intermediate associations. The hatred, envy, and jealousy we feel in adolescence and adulthood, along with the drive to kill, are largely neurotic derivatives and transferences of the patricidal sexual jealousy we feel towards our own father. Or, mutatis mutandis for females, the matricidal sexual jealousy we feel towards our own mother.

However, the child's sexual jealousy does not stop the child from identifying with the father, taking the father as an ideal model to imitate, as a means, perhaps *the* means, of winning the approval of the mother and thereby gaining sexual possession of the mother. In fact, this identification with the father is directly caused by the child's sexual jealousy towards the father, since it is the sexual jealousy which suggests that the father is the ideal model to imitate. The fantasy of vanity, winning social approval, is a distortion of the unconscious fantasy of winning the father's approval, which means the fantasy of completing the identification with and imitation of the father and thereby taking the father's place as the mother's lover. The wish to win the father's approval also takes the more personal form of the subject consulting his own conscience, or superego, in the privacy of his own mind. Clearly, in each case a different aspect of the Oedipus complex has predominance; for instance, either the sexual desire for the mother, the jealous hatred of the father, the identification with the father, the wish to win the father's approval, or castration anxiety (there are other elements of the Oedipus complex and its repression which we have not mentioned at length in this analysis). Changing the value of each element of the Oedipus complex results in a different variant of the Oedipus complex and thus a different variant of neurosis. However, in each case the Oedipus complex and primal repression remain constant as the structure of the unconscious mind. We may also describe the structure of the unconscious as the *character structure* of the individual, roughly corresponding to what in former times was described as the individual's character, humour, or temperament (e.g. in the writings of the French moralists, especially La Rochefoucauld, Montaigne, and Nicolas Chamfort, who were also psychologists par excellence, and from whom we have much to learn today).

In *On the Genealogy of Morals*, Nietzsche proposes slavery as the socio-historical explanation for the origin of ressentiment, and as a consequence he theorizes that there are two basic forms of morality which form the basis of two corresponding forms of society, namely master morality, which is devoid of ressentiment, and slave morality, which is produced by ressentiment. The ideal models for master morality are the pagan civilizations of the Greeks and the Romans, whereas the ideal model for slave morality is Christian civilization. However, in the light of our finding that ressentiment is universal due to the universality of the Oedipus complex and primal repression, it is evident that Nietzsche's theory of master morality and slave morality is untenable. It is clear that each individual and each society suffers from ressentiment, albeit to different degrees. We can clearly identify revenge fantasies even in the pagan religion of the Greeks and Romans, for example in the karmic justice enacted by the Furies and in the post-mortem punishments doled out by Hades in the kingdom of the dead. However, it is also abundantly clear, as pointed out by Nietzsche, that the Christian religion suffers from a severe and pathological case of ressentiment, as evinced by its concept of Hell, which is indubitably a revenge fantasy with a prime place of importance in the Christian religion. Therefore, although the moralities and cultures of the pagan Greco-Romans and the Christians both have their origins and their life in the Oedipus complex and primal repression, they are nonetheless two very distinct forms of the Oedipus complex, the pagan Greco-Romans being an ideal model a relatively healthy Oedipal morality and culture (i.e. a relatively healthy form of neurosis), whereas Christianity is the ideal model of a severe and toxic Oedipal morality and culture (i.e. a severe and toxic form of neurosis). Whereas the pagan Greco-Romans had an Oedipus complex which emphasized love for the mother and identification with the father (hence the worship of goddesses, particularly the goddess of love, Aphrodite, and the worship of heroes such as Hercules and Odysseus), Christians have a neurosis which emphasizes castration anxiety, ressentiment, and the super-ego (hence the concepts of original sin and Hell, as well as the self-debasement and self-humiliation as a form of worshipping the monotheistic and jealous God). We agree with Nietzsche that in addition to Christianity, anti-Semitism and racism generally are also examples of severe and toxic ressentiment, which in Freudian terminology means severe and toxic neurosis. In the *Science of Self-Actualization* (Kasem 2018, pp. 226-230), we identified fascism as the product of ressentiment, and we also linked with the ressentiment of Christianity the Christian fascism of the Nazis and American fascists (which includes Trump supporters, the KKK, American neo-Nazis, the far-right, the American right generally, the Republican party, and most Evangelical Christians). Here we add, in the light of the findings of psychoanalysis, that the severe and toxic form of ressentiment which characterizes racism and fascism is a severe and toxic form of neurosis which has its roots in a severe and toxic form of the Oedipus complex. Racism and fascism are symptoms of mental illness, meaning that in addition to being political problems they are primarily mental health problems, and the only way to permanently destroy them is to cure the underlying neurosis which causes them. In this regard, psychoanalysis is an essential weapon in the fight against fascism and racism.

We have mentioned above that repression is caused by the imposition of the incest taboo, and that Freud calls this process castration anxiety. The phrase "castration anxiety" must not be taken too literally. In the beginning of his essay "The Passing of the Oedipus Complex," Freud himself notes that there are various events which could result in the repression of the Oedipus complex, e.g. enduring a harsh punishment, the birth of a new sibling, or the death of the mother, the common ground among all these events being that they are painful experiences that occasion a deep disappointment, and that "reflection deepens the effect of these impressions by insisting that painful experiences of this kind, antagonistic to the contents of the complex, are inevitable" (1924, p. 269). In other words, the child experiences a trauma, and this trauma writes a new memory which represses the Oedipal drive. In the prototypical scenario that Freud outlines for the male child, the male child is threatened with castration if he persists in the activity of masturbation, the fantasy content which drives his masturbation being his sexual desire to possess his mother. Freud admits that "our insight into these processes of development in the girl is unsatisfying, shadowy and incomplete" (ibid, p. 275), but he nonetheless conjectures a prototypical scenario in which the female child, who has hitherto thought of herself as a male, discovers that the male sexual organ is different from hers, and to explain this traumatic discovery, she, with the logic of a child, believes that she once possessed a penis but was castrated; such is the prototype of penis envy in the female child, the female analogue of castration anxiety. However, Torok, in her essay "The Meaning of "Penis Envy" in Women," she presents a different prototypical model of penis envy; she argues that penis envy develops in a manner more similar to castration anxiety, to be more specific she argues that penis envy is caused when the female child is discovered masturbating by the mother and threatened with punishment, whereupon she grows envious of the privilege she conjectures that males must have (1994, pp. 41-73). We accept Freud's model of castration anxiety and Torok's model of penis envy as the prototypical cases of primal repression; they outline the manner in which primal repression is effected in the majority of men and women. We emphasize that although, following Freud, we describe psychosexual development overwhelmingly in terms of the prototypical male child, that is to say in terms of castration anxiety and the Oedipus complex, our conclusions apply mutatis mutandis to the female child, her penis envy, and her Electra complex.

Freud's theory of primal repression is not only perfectly compatible with Nietzsche's theory of the mnemonics of cruelty, but we can clearly see how the mnemonics of cruelty of the trauma of castration anxiety directly causes primal repression. Nietzsche's principle of the mnemonics of cruelty is that the greater the pain inflicted by the event, the greater its memorability. Trauma is an event so painful that it occupies the mind to the exclusion of what existed in the mind before it, in other words, trauma represses what came before it; Nietzsche, too, suggests this when he writes that bad conscience is produced by the fearful bulwarks of a political organization, meaning predominantly a system of punishment, repressing the old drives of freedom. Traumatization causes primal repression. The secondary repression of painful stimuli associated or resonant with the Oedipal drive regards stimuli which are painful but not traumatic, and is predicated upon the more primary experience of primal repression, which is itself effected by traumatization. Gradually, as the child becomes habituated to the trauma of castration anxiety, castration anxiety becomes automatized and implicit, but nonetheless active, in a process analogous to and closely linked with language acquisition; however, castration anxiety, i.e. the incest taboo, is never entirely forgotten and remains partially accessible to consciousness over the course of the individual's lifetime. This is evinced by the fact that one's existence as a member of society, one's social life, love life, fantasy life, and mating habits, are almost entirely predicated upon the incest taboo, which is largely implicit, although it can and does sometimes enter into consciousness, however briefly; the thought of the incest taboo is often too highly emotionally charged for the subject to contemplate it for too long, let alone rationally. Typically, contemplating the incest taboo stimulates the repressed Oedipal drive, which results in swift secondary repression and the reinforcement of primal repression by the repressive drive, and thus the inability to contemplate the incest taboo rationally or at length. We agree with the anthropologist Lévi-Strauss that the incest taboo is both universal in humanity and a cultural acquisition, and in the light of our findings and the findings of Freud, we agree with Freud's conclusion that the Oedipus complex is universal in humankind, and we also conclude that the incest taboo is universal because primal repression is universal.

In *Beyond the Pleasure Principle*, Freud describes trauma as an excessive influx of excitations which is "powerful enough to break through the protective shield" of the perceptual apparatus (1961, p. 23). Although he conceived of the perceptual apparatus as equivalent to consciousness, we will consider his statement here in the light of our finding that the perceptual apparatus is unconscious. We argue that the "protective shield" of the perceptual apparatus discussed by Freud is in fact the protective armour of defence mechanisms predicated upon primal repression, all the mechanisms of secondary repression predicated upon primal repression. Following Wilhelm Reich, we recognize that this psychological armour is simultaneously physical, meaning that this protective armour of defence mechanisms is inscribed in the body, including the sensory organs, hence the protective shield of the perceptual apparatus. However, it is evident that prior to primal repression the perceptual apparatus has no such protective armour. Indeed, in infancy and early childhood, the child is exceedingly sensitive, impressionable, and vulnerable, and this is because the system Pcpt-Ucs of the child, which has not yet undergone primal repression, has no protective barrier of defence mechanisms. Psychedelic drugs temporarily render inoperative the psycho-somatic armour of defence mechanisms in the system Pcpt-Ucs, hence the child-like sensitivity, impressionability, and vulnerability of the individual undergoing the psychedelic experience (the ingestion of drugs, like the ingestion of music, is the ingestion of raw drives of varying colours or timbres, raw affects devoid of content, which activate signifying-chains in the system Ucs with resonant or associated affects). Therefore, prior to primal repression, the child, being much more emotionally vulnerable, is also much more susceptible to experiencing trauma; indeed, it is this very vulnerability which allows the trauma of castration anxiety to effect primal repression. After having experienced primal repression, the system Pcpt-Ucs of the child constructs a protective barrier of defence mechanisms. By means of this protective barrier, any perceptions which are associated with or resonant with the repressed Oedipal drive are likewise repressed, usually via the defence mechanism of denial. Thus, any subsequent trauma occurs in the manner described by Freud, as an excessive influx of excitations which are powerful enough to break through the protective shield of the system Pcpt-Ucs. Typically, this new trauma is a new drive whose conditions of production are antithetical to both the repressive incest-taboo drive and the repressed Oedipal drive, which means for the subject that neurotic unpleasures increase exponentially, conflicts between the organism's drives and the new trauma rapidly proliferate, and it becomes exponentially more difficult to acquire or even to fantasize about the quasi-pleasures necessary to sustain the repressed Oedipal drive which is the very core of the human organism, meaning that as a consequence the entire organism is drained of its energy, resulting in the loss of the desire to live and the physical inactivity characteristic of patients suffering from melancholia, thus putting the human organism at risk of death, not only by suicide as a desperate means to end this state of exponential torment devoid even of quasi-pleasures, but also at risk of death by sheer melancholia, that is to say, through the extreme depletion of biological energy.

Freud writes that primal repression operates by means of a *reaction-formation*, or *substitute-formation*, the intensification of an antithesis (1915, p. 96). It is clear to see that in the case of primal repression, the incest taboo is the antithesis of the Oedipus complex, thus the incest taboo is the reaction-formation, or substitute-formation, by means of which primal repression is effected. That the incest taboo is a substitute-formation for the Oedipus complex means that the incest taboo, as a taboo that must not be violated under any circumstances, is the object of desire of the repressive drive, which functions to perpetuates the incest taboo. Because the incest taboo is the substitute-formation for the Oedipus complex, sexual desire comes to be predicated on the incest taboo as a means of perpetuating the incest taboo, and it is for this reason that the subject seeks sexual partners other than the mother. The incest taboo is the repressive socius of fantasy. Sexual desire and its correlated object of desire are always, strictly speaking, Oedipal in nature, since the Oedipal drive always remains the core of the human organism, the engine which powers, ultimately, all psychical and physical activity. However, in the case of repression, only those fantasy-crystals (which we may also understand as energy-crystals) fabricated by the Oedipal drive become an effective driving force of the organism which pass the censorship of the repressive force, meaning only those Oedipal fantasy-crystals which are sufficiently enough removed from the original Oedipal fantasy due to their distortion or their number of intermediate associations (in other words, only those Oedipal fantasy-crystals that can be described as neurotic derivatives), thereby allowing them to be appropriated, consumed, and introjected or incorporated by the repressive force, overcoded with the inscriptions of the repressive socius of fantasy, the incest taboo, and thus re-produced as the object of desire of the repressive drive. We may describe such an object of desire as a *repressive object of desire* or a *neurotic object of desire*. The repressive object of desire is a means of satisfying both the repressive drive and the repressed Oedipal drive, which means that it has as its essential elements both the incest taboo and the sexual desire for the mother, and that it yields quasi-pleasure not only for the repressed Oedipal drive, but also quasi-pleasure, in addition to neurotic unpleasure, for the repressive drive. It is the production of neurotic objects of desire which explains our choice of sexual partners, who in a few essential ways resembles the object of our Oedipal desire (hence the erotic transference of feelings for the mother or father onto the neurotic object of desire), and yet in other ways, both in terms of physical appearance and personality traits, differs significantly from our Oedipal object of desire (viz. because the neurotic object of desire is a distortion of the Oedipal object of desire).

In *Beyond the Pleasure Principle*, Freud develops his theory of *repetition-compulsion*, the drive to repeat an earlier action. Freud conceives of repetition-compulsion as independent of and not governed by the pleasure principle, and he explains it in terms of the desire to return to an earlier state of things. We reject Freud's explanation of repetition-compulsion, although we recognize that it is a significant factor in the life of the drives. Freud provides evidence for the existence of repetition-compulsion by citing the behaviour of children at play, who often repeat their unpleasant experiences in play because the repetition carries "along with it a yield of pleasure of another sort but none the less a direct one" (1961, p. 10). We argue that repetition-compulsion is entirely explicable in terms of the pleasure principle, meaning that an action is repeated in the hope that it will bring pleasure, with the amendments of our structural and economic model of the unconscious, meaning that although an action inevitably fails to bring any pleasure, it may bring quasi-pleasure if it reproduces a drive's conditions of production, and so an action may be repeated because its repetition produces quasi-pleasure. In other words, repetition-compulsion is the repeated failure to possess the object of desire, a repetition of failure which nonetheless garners quasi-pleasures because it reproduces the given drive's mode of production, meaning that it allows the drive to continue fantasizing about possessing the object of desire. Here we owe a tremendous debt to Lacan, who writes that jouissance is produced by the repeated failure to attain the object of desire. Indeed, in our metapsychology, consciousness, which is jouissance, is indeed produced by the repeated failure to possess the object of desire. However, the repeated failure to possess the object of desire is more fundamental to desire since it is part of the very structure of desire, which by its very nature cannot be satisfied. In other words, repetition-compulsion is an essential element of desire, which is governed by the pleasure principle.

Moreover, the phenomenon of repetition-compulsion also suggests the process whereby a fantasy is encoded and a drive is formed. A fantasy is encoded by means of pain-excitations which double as quasi-pleasure because they reproduce the conditions of production. The greater the positive quantity of excitations, the greater the negative quantity of potentiality for pleasure. Therefore, the inscription of excitations, because each excitation is inextricable and coextensive with a potentiality for pleasure, is also the inscription of fantasy, and the activity correlated with the inscription of excitations is repeated compulsively in repeatedly failed attempts to possess the object of desire which has also been inscribed, but this repetition-compulsion nonetheless enables the drive to continue fantasizing about possessing the object of desire, thus garnering quasi-pleasures. Through this process of the encoding of fantasy, raw drive is transformed into a particular drive with a particular content, hence why we also describe this process as the formation of a drive. We may also describe this process of the formation of drives as the *grafting* of drives when the drive is formed due to excitations originating from the environment external to the organism. When the drive is formed due to excitations with origins internal to the organism, then it is not really the formation of a new drive as such, but merely the natural mechanism by which the fantasy-crystals produced by a drive's mode of crystallization become an object of desire for the drive to pursue. Grafting is the process whereby the raw drive of the infant and its erotogenic systems are inscribed with particular content, invariably a sociocultural and socio-political content, e.g. this is the process whereby the oral erotogenic system of the infant comes to desire the breast, the process whereby the anal erotogenic system of the infant comes to desire the with-holding and release of excrement, the process whereby the genital erotogenic system of the infant comes to desire the sexual possession of the mother, and the process whereby the genital erotogenic system of the infant represses its sexual desire for the mother. The economic problem of masochism has its solution precisely here: desire is essentially masochistic not only because it always yields pain, but also because it always actively desires pain as a means to pleasure, and although this pleasure is never something it actually experiences, desire does indeed garner quasi-pleasure from those pain-excitations which it actively desires since those pain-excitations reproduce its conditions of production. It is important to note that while the graftings of the oral drive, the anal drive, and the Oedipal drive are typically entirely benevolent and symbiotic, the grafting of primal repression is malignant and parasitic. This is because primal repression is an attempt, an inevitably failed attempt, to undo the Oedipal drive, despite the fact that the Oedipal drive has already become instinct, inscribed into the core of the body. The Oedipus complex is a sexual orientation and a paraphilia, meaning that the attempt of primal repression to undo it is already too late, always already too late, succeeding through traumatization only in repressing and distorting the Oedipus complex, but never succeeding in destroying or expelling it completely. Primal repression may be considered as an extreme and traumatic form of "conversion therapy" applied to the Oedipus complex, which, just like conversion therapy, is inhumane, cruel, and destined to fail.

Moreover, upon re-reviewing the physiological evidence, experimental evidence, and psychoanalytic theories we compiled in a previous volume (cf. *Whose Unconscious Is It?*, Kasem 2017, pp. 72-87; we mean in particular, Harlow and Zimmerman's experiments with macaques; Panksepp's neurophysiology of the attachment system, panic system, and the seeking system, corresponding roughly to the opioid system, opioid withdrawal system, and the dopamine system in the brain; and Bowlby's attachment theory), as well as new observations of *Homo sapiens* in natura and the review of literature we had not perused before, we conclude that psychosexual development does not occur in the exact manner described by Freud; to be more specific, we conclude that the male infant's sexual desire for the mother has its origin and continuation primarily in the entire nervous system (considered as an erotogenic zone or erotogenic system unto itself), and not in the manner that Freud thought, developing out of the oral erotogenic zone. Freud theorized that the male infant's sexual desire for the mother developed out of the infant's desire to suckle the mother's breasts and thereby acquire nourishment. However, Harlow and Zimmerman's (1959) famous study with infant macaques revealed that faced with the choice between two artificial surrogate mothers constructed by the researchers, a lactating wire-mother with a milk bottle and a non-lactating cloth-mother which was capable of being hugged but had no milk bottle, infant macaques had a clear preference for the huggable cloth-mother, which they even ran and clung to when faced with perceived danger. Due to the genetic similarity of humans and macaques, in addition to the observation of human infants, it is safe to conclude that the same applies to human infants as it does to macaques infants, namely that physical affection is more important than nourishment in the formation of an attachment bond with the primary caregiver. This suggests both that the entire body must be considered as an erotogenic zone, and more particularly, the entire peripheral nervous system, which is the very organ of touch, must be considered as an erotogenic zone, and that sexual desire consists primarily of attachment and panic (the lack of the object of attachment). Harlow and Zimmerman's experiments with macaques clearly reveal the truth of the ancient adage that for humans, love is more important than food; or, to state it more sacrilegiously, but just as anciently, sex is more important than food.

Fink writes, "Taking Freud's notion of polymorphous perversity to the extreme, we can view the infant's body as one unbroken erogenous zone, there being no privileged zones, no areas in which pleasure is circumscribed at the outset" (1996, p. 24). Freud himself writes that the mother inadvertently sexually arouses her child by caressing him all over his body (despite the care she takes to avoid caressing his genitals, since sexual arousal can and does occur by way of stimulating areas of the body other than the genitals); Freud writes that the mother, although she regards her love for her child as "pure love," unbeknownst to herself regards the child "with feelings that are derived from her own sexual life: she strokes him, kisses him, rocks him and quite clearly treats him as a substitute for a complete sexual object" (Freud, 1962; as quoted in Nasio, 2005/2010, p. 1). Freud writes that the mother's physical contact with her child is in effect sexual seduction; by touching her child all over his body, the mother arouses in the child a number of pleasurable physical sensations, thus by her care of her child's body the mother becomes her child's first seducer (1940, p. 188). Considering that Freud writes of the polymorphous perversity of the infant's body and the sexual arousal of the child by means of his mother caressing him all over his body, Freud himself gives us the means to go beyond his theory of the "oral stage" of psychosexual development, since he gives us a clear indication of the vast importance that tactile stimulation all over the body has in the child's psychosexual development. This supports Fink's observation that the infant's body is one unbroken erogenous zone. We argue that the peripheral nervous system, the very organ of touch, must be considered as an erogenous zone, or erotogenic zone, unto itself; moreover, we argue that the peripheral nervous system is the primary erotogenic zone in psychosexual development. To be sure, the oral zone, anal zone, and genital zone are only erotogenic zones insofar as they contain nerve-endings which are capable of being stimulated. However, the peripheral nervous system is distributed throughout the unbroken erotogenic zone that is the body, and to designate specifically the organ of the body equivalent to this unbroken erotogenic zone, we identify the peripheral nervous system, the organ of touch. Distinguishing the peripheral nervous system as an erotogenic zone also accounts for the fact that the vast regions of the body remain erotogenic zones even after erotic pleasure becomes localized in specific areas of the body. Considered as an erotogenic system, i.e. as a desiring-machine, the peripheral nervous system, just like the mouth, ingests psychosemiotic flows which are simultaneously material flows in order to acquire quasi-pleasures. Considering the entire peripheral nervous system as an erotogenic system accounts for the fact that the child's desire to possess the mother is primarily a desire of the whole body of the child for the whole body of the mother, which originates from the whole body of the child and in which the whole body continues playing a vital role. This means that not only the Oedipus complex, but primal repression as well, is inscribed into the entire peripheral nervous system. Therefore, the acquisition of sexuality is similar to the acquisition of language, coincides with the acquisition of language, and is indeed closely linked with the acquisition of language. Sexuality is the language of touch, as it were, and the critical period for acquiring this language of touch is the same as that of acquiring natural language. Moreover, the acquisition of sexuality takes several years, and it involves the acquisition not only of the Oedipus complex, but of primal repression as well, both of which thereupon constitute essential elements of an individual's sexuality. To be sure, acquiring the language of sexuality means acquiring a syntax of sexuality as well as a vocabulary of sexuality. This syntax of sexuality is also the syntax of culture, society, thought, and behaviour, and just as Chomsky argued that the syntax of language is a generative grammar that accounts for the production of new sentences, we argue that the syntax of sexuality accounts for the production of new thoughts and behaviours.

In terms of neurophysiological systems, this means that the sex drive has as its primary neurobiological correlates the attachment system and the panic system, which most prominently involves the opioid neurotransmitters and their withdrawal, and only secondarily has as its neurobiological correlate the seeking system, which most prominently involves the neurotransmitter dopamine. In discussing the attachment system, panic system, and seeking system, we largely draw upon the Panksepp's neurophysiology of emotions (Panksepp, 1998). The child's attachment bond to the object of attachment, the primary caregiver, is a constant feeling of bliss caused by the constant reproduction of the conditions of production, and the neurobiological correlate of this is the attachment system, which constantly releases opioids in the brain while the child is near the presence of the object of attachment. The panic system is opiod withdrawal, the inverse of the attachment system, and it is triggered by the loss, whether temporary or permanent, of the object of attachment. The panic system is also sometimes called the separation-distress system. When the lack of the object of attachment initially stimulates the panic system, the panic system in turn stimulates the seeking system and its correlated seeking behaviours, for instance searching the environment for the object of attachment and producing distress-vocalizaitons, indubitably in the hopes of finding or being found by the object of attachment. However, if the panic system continues being stimulated for a longer period of time due to the continued absence of the object of attachment, this seeking behaviour then turns into withdrawal behaviour, the animal withdraws from the environment, retreating into isolation and experiencing acute melancholia (cf. Solms and Turnbull, 2002, pp. 130-131). This biphasic panic response, which moves from the seeking phase to the withdrawal phase, corresponds precisely to the "biphasic protest-despair response" of separation anxiety discovered by Bowlby (1969). We theorize that it is the repeated experience of separation anxiety and its attendant panic during early childhood, which is to a degree inevitable, whether temporarily or permanently, and during which the seeking system is activated, that, due to its intensity and thus its high quantity of excitations, sets the foundation for the seeking quality of sexual desire and its attendant seeking behaviour, which must be understood as essentially a panic response triggered by the lack of the object of attachment (with its neurobiological correlates, the activation of the panic system and its attendant opioid withdrawal, and the simultaneous activation of the seeking system and its dopamine circuit). At first, the absence of the child's object of attachment, i.e. the absence of the child's mother, and his attendant separation anxiety, are usually caused circumstantially and accidentally, for instance when the mother needs to leave the room, or when the mother has to leave the child with a babysitter because she has to go to work. However, as a result of the repression of the Oedipus complex, the repressed Oedipal drive, cut off from the external world, experiences the loss of the object of attachment, which triggers the first phase of the panic response, the proliferation of neurotic derivatives of the Oedipal object of desire, some of which pass the censorship of the repressive drive and thus direct the perceptual apparatus, meaning that the organism performs the seeking behaviours characteristic of desire. Bowlby's theory of attachment styles, namely that there are four main types of attachment bonds and their corresponding modes of responding to separation (viz. secure, avoidant, ambivalent, and disorganized), is comprehensively researched and well argued, and it has been well-documented that these attachment styles become ingrained in the subject, characterizing all of a given individual's romantic attachments. Each attachment style is caused by a corresponding type of primary caregiver, a personality type which recurs as the same personality type of the subject's romantic partners later in life (e.g. a distant and disengaged mother creates a child with an avoidant attachment style, meaning that the child is likewise emotionally distant). We argue that the repression of the Oedipus complex is the mechanism which accounts for the transference of attachment styles onto new others of desire, since it is also the mechanism whereby the attachment bond is transferred onto new others of desire, who become, due to erotic transference, new objects of attachment. The object of desire is that which we seek out but never find, what we find in actuality is the other of desire, who becomes the object of attachment with whom we forge an attachment bond.

We find the universal existence of the Oedipus complex in males, and the Electra complex in females, to be certain beyond a reasonable doubt. We add that gender is biological in origin and that the primary physiological organ it involves is the brain. We accept Proust's account of homosexuality, or "inversion" (as it was once called, perhaps more accurately), as outlined in *Sodom and Gomorrah*, the fourth volume of his novel *In Search of Lost Time* (1981/1993). Proust writes that homosexual males are essentially women in men's bodies, while homosexual females are essentially men in women's bodies. Proust's theory of sexual inversion is supported by modern neurobiology. Savic and Lindstrom (2008) found that the brains of homosexual men resembled those of heterosexual women, while the brains of homosexual women resembled those of heterosexual men. Inversion is not merely a matter of sexual orientation, since it is primarily a matter of gender. We agree with Freud that there is an inherently bisexual dimension of the libido; however, it is overwhelmingly clear that sexual orientation is biologically determined and not acquired in early childhood, except in the case of paraphilias (but even with paraphilias there are ambiguities, since there are undeniably biological predispositions to acquiring a paraphilia). To clarify, inversion is not a paraphilia, but a natural sexual orientation resulting from the gender of the brain. The brain is sexed due to a combination of genetics and the conditions experienced in utero, and its sexuation must be considered in terms of dimensionality; viz. there are two dimensions of gender, male and female, and the degree to which the brain is male or female is determined by a combination of genetics and in utero conditions. There may be a high degree of both masculinity and femininity of the brain, which would mean that the brain is hermaphroditic. Considering gender as physiological dimensions of the brain can also help account for other gender orientations, such as transgender. The implication for psychoanalysis is that the young child's sexual preference for either the mother or the father is biologically determined, such that heterosexual men and homosexual women develop the Oedipus complex, whereas heterosexual women and homosexual men develop the Electra complex.

A further implication for both psychoanalysis and neuroscience is that the brain must be considered not only as the neurobiological correlate of metapsychological structures, but as ultimately a metapsychological structure unto itself. In other words, the brain is an erotogenic system, or erotogenic zone, unto itself. Flows of neurotransmitters are also flows of libido. The metapsychological structure of the brain can be modelled in several different ways: the brain as a whole can be considered as a single desiring-machine, each functional system of the brain can be considered as a desiring-machine, or each individual neuron can be considered as a desiring-machine. Although this would be a fruitful field of inquiry, there remains numerous ambiguities here; for instance, a single metapsychological system may have as its biological correlate several different but interrelated physiological systems, and vice versa. Moreover, since it is evident that many of the metapsychological systems we have discussed have important neurobiological correlates in the brain, the complex relationships between these metapsychological systems, their neurobiological correlates, and the brain considered as metapsychological system unto itself must be clarified. The intersection of psychoanalysis, post-structural philosophy, and neuroscience would be helpful not only in understanding gender and sexual orientation, but also in numerous other, different ways, for example understanding and treating drug addiction. Drug addiction is a physiological addiction of the brain, and this may be understood in terms of the desiring-machines of the brain having a need to ingest a chemical flow which is also a flow of libido, and this in turn can be related to the needs of other identifiable desiring-machines in the unconscious; for example, opioid addiction can be analysed in this way, with on the one hand analysing the desiring-machines of the brain needing chemical-libidinal flows of opioids, and on the other hand analysing the genital desiring-machine and the peripheral nervous system desiring-machine in terms of their perceived loss of the object of attachment, their consequent panic, and their neurobiological correlate, the panic system. It is evident that the subject's repressed Oedipal drive moving from the protest phase to the despair phase of separation anxiety (no doubt occasioned by some external circumstance, for instance being left by one's lover) and the resulting melancholia, or depression, leads to opioid addiction, whereupon the desiring-machine of the brain pathologically craves the ingestion of flows of opioids from the environment, ultimately in order to acquire quasi-pleasures for the repressed Oedipal drive (according to our earlier conclusions, in a form which also acquires quasi-pleasures for the repressive drive). Thus the treatment of opioid addiction must be two-fold: on the one hand, the subject must undergo a physiological and chemical treatment in order to cure his physiological addiction, and on the other hand the subject must undergo a psychoanalytic treatment to cure the ultimate cause of his opioid addiction, which is, strictly speaking, psychological and emotional in nature.

We support the use of psychedelic drugs as a means of treating mental illness and addiction, based on the findings of numerous researchers (cf. Tupper et al. 2015; Amoroso 2015; Schenberg 2018; Grof 1996). The psychedelic experience often results in the experiencer feeling transformed, renewed, and rejuvenated, and even reborn, according to the first-hand reports of test subjects and psychedelic drug users (cf. Hoffman 1979/1983; Huxley 1954/2009; Rios and Janiger 2003). We have concluded that the transformation of consciousness effected by the psychedelic experience is caused by the transformation of the unconscious. We add that the medicinal use of psychedelic drugs must be preceded by and followed by sessions of psychoanalysis, for at least several weeks in advance and several weeks following, and that it must be chaperoned by a psychoanalyst who serves, as it were, as the shaman or guide for the patient, in order for the psychedelic treatment to have maximal effect. It goes without saying that the psychoanalyst must himself use the psychedelic drug in question and undergo the psychedelic experience at least three times in order to responsibly, efficiently, and successfully chaperone the patient.

However, what exactly would constitute a cure? More specifically, what exactly would constitute a cure for neurosis? Since neurosis is produced by primal repression, the cure for neurosis lies precisely in the abrogation of primal repression. Maintaining the repression of the Oedipal drive means maintaining neurosis. In other words, the parasitic repressive drive must be excised from the host organism in order to cure neurosis. Primal repression is maintained by means of the trauma of castration anxiety. Castration anxiety is a trauma inscribed upon and circumscribing the very core of being. This primal trauma must be treated and healed so that the patient ceases to constantly live in fear of punishment. First, the analysand must be put in touch with the core of his being, the Oedipal drive, which must be put directly in touch with the external world. It is only then, at the level of dealing directly with the Oedipal drive, that the Oedipus complex can become truly resolved. The Oedipus complex can be truly resolved, or deconstructed, by means of being put in touch with raw drive, the energy which drives the core of being; this can be done realizing the difference between the object of desire and the other of desire, and thus also realizing that desire can never be truly satisfied; it is only by this means that the analysand can be put in touch with the raw drive at the ultimate core of his being, which is the polymorphous perversity of being and desire. One must take off the mask of Oedipus in order to become the supreme actor, Dionysus, he who wears all masks. Because raw drive is suffering, this means cultivating hardiness. Mental health consists not in never feeling suffering, but in being able to endure suffering. Hardiness is mental health.

Deleuze and Guattari write that social production, the production of society, is determined by desiring-production: "We maintain that the social field is immediately invested by desire, that it is the historically determined product of desire" (1972/1977, p. 29). Taking our findings into account, this means that each type of society has its own characteristic types of the unconscious—its own characteristic types of the Oedipus complex, primal repression, and repressive drive—which produce and reproduce that type of society. For instance, capitalist society has two main types of unconscious, that of the bourgeoisie, who is the entrepreneur and thus the capitalist as such, and that of the proletariat, who is both consumer and exploited labourer.

Desiring-machines are fantasy machines or dream-machines, and it is on the basis of its fantasies that desiring-machines act upon the Real and construct the Real. Although desiring-production primarily produces fantasies, the forces of desiring-production and their relations to other forces and systems of desiring-production in the environment are proto-Real, and therefore desiring-production always produces effects upon the proto-Real, meaning that although desiring-production is to a large extent circumscribed by the proto-Real, desiring-production also constructs the proto-Real to an equally large extent. E.g. although the bourgeoisie and the proletariat are overwhelmingly born into their respective social classes, and thus condemned by birth to be either a bourgeois or a proletariat, the type of unconscious they acquire in turn produce, maintain, and reproduce the social system into which they were born. Deleuze and Guattari write that Wilhelm Reich remarks that "the astonishing thing is not that some people steal or that others occasionally go out on strike, but rather that all those who are starving do not steal as a regular practice, and all those who are exploited are not continually out on strike" (ibid, p. 29). What prevents the exploited proletariat from rebelling against the system that exploits him? Why does the proletariat instead maintain and perpetuate the very society that exploits him? We have concluded that it is the unconscious of the proletariat which determines his existence as a proletariat as such, as opposed to a career criminal or a revolutionary. The same applies, mutatis mutandis, to the bourgeoisie, who continue exploiting the proletariat instead of trying to transform society. The unconscious of John Dillinger differs significantly from and is much healthier than the unconscious of the average proletariat. The unconscious of Che Guevara differs significantly from and is much healthier than the unconscious of the average bourgeois.

Deleuze and Guattari also describe society as the *social machine* (ibid, pp. 139-145). Society, considered as a machine, is a system of flows and interruptions of flows. In the light of our findings, a social machine consists not only of an individual's masochistic machines, lack-machine, and sensual machine, but of the masochistic machines, lack-machines, and sensual machines of several individuals, functioning together as a single unit, however dysfunctional this functioning may be. Deleuze and Guattari write, "The fact there is massive social repression that has an enormous effect on desiring-production in no way vitiates our principle: desire produces reality, or stated another way, desiring-production is one and the same thing as social production" (ibid, p. 30). We understand desiring-production's production of reality in a different sense than Deleuze and Guattari; as we wrote above, desiring-production primarily produces fantasies, and as a result of producing fantasies it secondarily produces, on the one hand, the reality of consciousness as its surplus value, and on the other hand, real effects upon the Real and the proto-Real. It is in this sense that we identify desiring-production and social production to be one and the same process of production. Moreover, it is evident that social repression and psychic repression are one and the same thing. The psychic repression of the Oedipus complex is always already social repression. In fact, it is the incest taboo which forms the basis of society, which means that it is primal repression which forms the basis of society.

The social machine is an intelligent machine, not only because its component machines are intelligent machines, but also because its intelligence emerges out of the interaction of its component machines as if it were a surplus entity distinct from the individuals which compose it, exactly in the manner of *swarm intelligence* described by biologists and computer scientists. William S. Burroughs wrote that when two minds collaborate, a "third mind" emerges which governs their collaboration; this is exactly the kind of phenomenon we denote with our concept of the swarm intelligence of the social machine. The "third mind" is the swarm intelligence of a social machine which consists of two individuals. A single individual is already, in a sense, a swarm intelligence and a social machine, since he is composed of a multiplicity of intelligent machines which function together as a single unit; however, for pragmatic purposes we reserve the use of the phrases "swarm intelligence" and "social machine" for the relatively more traditional sense of the term, which refers to a group of individuals (two being the minimum number of individuals necessary to constitute a social machine). Each society is a social machine endowed with swarm intelligence.

An excellent analogy for the swarm intelligence of human beings is the swarm intelligence of social insects, and just as with the intelligence of the individual unconscious, the swarm intelligence of the group unconscious can be more easily understood by drawing analogies with plant intelligence. Explaining the similarities between the swarm intelligence of social insects and plant intelligence, Trewavas (2006, p. 12) writes, "Not only are there numerous exploratory trails or flights to find rich resources, but, once discovered, changes in colony communication ensure numerous individuals (like proliferating leaves or branch roots) are actively employed in resource acquisition. The whole system benefits by the changes in foraging form. Bell (1984) has drawn analogies between plant branching and the foraging system of ants. The plant phenotype is constructed to benefit the whole organism using environmental signals that are internally assessed against current and previous experience." Foucault discovered that each society is a form of domination. In the light of our findings, we understand this in metapsychological terms: each society is a form of domination because it is, at bottom, a psychical mode of production and a psychical ideological apparatus, meaning that each society is driven by a fantasy produced by each of its members and that it strives through each of its members to reproduce the conditions of producing this fantasy. The members of a society are human beings who, through numerous exploratory trails, find rich psychosemiotic and material resources; and once these psychosemiotic and material resources are discovered, acts of communication ensure that numerous individuals, like ants or proliferating branch roots, are actively employed in the acquisition of these psychosemiotic and material resources. This means that metapsychological structures within a given individual are constructed to benefit the entire social machine, i.e. in the service of the increased domination of the social machine.

The mode of production of a society is ultimately a psychical mode of production, that is to say, the production of fantasy; each social machine has its characteristic fantasy, which is produced and reproduced in and through the desiring-production of individuals. Even when a social machine is constituted by different types of unconscious with different types of fantasy, as it so often is, there is still at bottom an essential element of fantasy that they all share, and it is precisely this shared element of fantasy, which we may describe as the *group fantasy* or *collective fantasy* (or the *group socius of fantasy*, or the *collective socius of fantasy*), which binds them together as members of the same society and as components of the same social machine. For example, the bourgeoisie and the proletariat are united by the fantasy of capital, which drives their collaborative, integrated functioning in the social machine of capitalism; the fantasy of capital is the group socius of fantasy of the capitalist social machine, the group fantasy of capitalism. The group socius of fantasy is also what enables males and females, with their respective Oedipus complexes and Electra complexes, to function together in the same social system, even in cases where the social system in question oppresses, subjugates, and exploits the females which constitute roughly one half of its members.

We believe that the overarching aim of psychoanalysis ought to be planetary healing, healing the entirety of human civilization, which means the construction of a new society which produces and reproduces mental health by producing and reproducing a healthy unconscious, one devoid of primal repression and thus devoid of neurosis, secondary repressions, neurotic unpleasure, and ressentiment. In regard to this field of inquiry, this topic has been explored in the following works: *Life Against Death: The Psychoanalytical Meaning of History* by Norman O. Brown (1959/1985), *Eros and Civilization: A Philosophical Inquiry into Freud* by Herbert Marcuse (1955/1966), and *The Mass Psychology of Fascism* by Wilhelm Reich (1980). An outline of this utopian project in the light of our new psychoanalytic findings remains to be made, but it is an imperative line of inquiry. Civilization as it is, with its discontents, is diseased with neurosis, and systemically produces and reproduces the disease of neurosis. Moreover, we conclude that the cause of the climate emergency, which threatens the survival of the entire human species in the near future, is ultimately caused by psychological factors, namely the neuroses characterizing capitalist society. Therefore, the mass application, or mass production, of psychoanalysis is urgently required. It is only by healing the human race that mass action can be taken against the climate emergency. Pragmatically, this means on the one hand the mass application of psychedelic psychoanalytic therapy, which can be performed en masse by gathering together a large group of people in one location and administering psychedelic drugs to them while they experience a music concert, play, or film screening, chaperoned by designated psychoanalysts; on the other hand, it means the production of new cultural artefacts (viz. music, plays, films, paintings, books) in order to produce a new culture, one based on new, healthier values, which in turn will produce new, healthier human beings. It is the categorical imperative of the artist today to be a shaman, or healer, and this can be done by applying psychoanalysis to the arts, such that a code of symbols leads the spectator back to the core of being.

Following Freud, we believe that an important key to this artistic problem is our dreams. Freud wrote in *The Interpretation of Dreams* that "dreams are the royal road to the unconscious," which means for us that recording our dreams, transforming our dreams into works of art and literature, is a significant and easily accessible method of performing psychoanalytic shamanism in the arts. Our dreams are the products of the system Ucs while we sleep, meaning while our system Pcpt-Ucs is mostly cut off from the external world, therefore during our dreams we are closer to our repressed unconscious drive (despite the dream censorship performed by the repressive drive) than in our waking hours, during which the repressive drive is more connected to the external world and thus more dominant. In addition, we also believe in inducing hallucinations in ourselves by means of psychedelic drugs, and thereupon either producing works of art while in a hallucinatory, emotionally vulnerable psychedelic state, or transcribing later, when sober, the visions we received during the psychedelic experience. The psychedelic experience is another important key in our task. The third important key to our task is the autobiographical novel, especially in the vein of Henry Miller, Louis-Ferdinand Céline, Marcel Proust, and Jack Kerouac. On the one hand, the autobiographical novel is an invaluable psychological document of free association, and on the other hand the autobiographical novelist is a psychologist in his own right, providing us with new observations on the self and the other, new observations on human society, and new insights into the nature of the human psyche. These three methods of artistic production are the three keys to the problem of producing a new, healthier culture, and it is the categorical imperative of the artist today to employ them. We may describe our artistic philosophy as *oneirology*, and we may describe the artists who practice it as *oneirologists*.

References

Adkins, B. (2015). *Deleuze and Guattari's A Thousand Plateaus: A Critical Introduction and Guide*. Edinburgh: Edinburgh University Press

Allmann, J.M. (1999). Evolving brains. Scientific American Library, New York

Althusser, Louis. (2001). *Lenin and Philosophy and other essays*. (Ben Brewster, trans.). New York, NY: Monthly Review Press

Amoroso, T. (2015). "The Psychopharmacology of ±3,4 Methylenedioxymethamphetamine and its Role in the Treatment of Posttraumatic Stress Disorder". *Journal of Psychoactive Drugs*, *47* (5): 337–44.

Baluška, F., Mancuso, S., Volkmann, D. (Eds.). (2006). *Communication in Plants: Neuronal Aspects of Plant Life*. Berlin & Heidelberg: Springer-Verlag

Barbieri, M. (Ed.). (2007). *Introduction to Biosemiotics: The New Biological Synthesis*. Dordrecht: Springer

Bataille, G. (1945/1992). *On Nietzsche* (Bruce Boone, trans.). London: Paragon House

Bell, A.D. (1984). "Dynamicmorphology: a contribution to plant population ecology". In: R. Dirzo, J. Sarukhan (Eds.), *Perspectives on Plant Population Ecology*. Sunderland: Sinauer, pp. 48–65

Bijisma, J.J.E. & Groisman, E.A. (2003). Making informed decisions: regulatory interactions between two component systems. *Trends Microbiol*, 11: 359–366

Bowlby, J. (1969). *Attachment and Loss Volume 1: Attachment* (1st ed.). Basic Books

Brown, N.O. (1959/1985). *Life Against Death: The Psychoanalytical Meaning of History*. Middletown: Wesleyan University Press

Chomsky, N. (1959). "A Review of B.F. Skinner's *Verbal Behaviour*". In A. Arnove (Ed.), *The Essential Chomsky* (2008, pp. 1-30). New York: The New Press

Deleuze, G. (1962/1983). *Nietzsche and Philosophy*. (Hugh Tomlinson, trans.). New York: Columbia University Press

Deleuze, G. (1964/1972). *Proust and Signs*. (Richard Howard, trans.). Minneapolis, MN: University of Minnesota Press

Deleuze, G. and Guattari, F. (1972/1977). *Anti-Oedipus*. (Robert Hurley, Mark Seem, and Helen R. Lane, trans.). New York:

Penguin Books

Deleuze, G. & Guattari, F. (1980/1987). *A Thousand Plateaus* (Brian Massumi, trans.). London: University of Minnesota Press.

Derrida, J. (1997). *Of Grammatology*. (Gayatri Spivak, trans.). Baltimore and London: The John Hopkins University Press

Derrida, J. (1979). *Spurs: Nietzsche's Styles* (Barbara Harlow, trans.). Chicago: University of Chicago Press

Descartes, R. (2010). *Meditations* (Desmond M. Clarke, trans.). London: Penguin Books

Fink, B. (1996). *The Lacanian Subject.* Princeton: Princeton University Press

Freud, S. (1915). "Repression". In E. Jones (Ed.), J. Riviere (trans.), *Sigmund Freud, Collected Papers, Volume IV* (1959, pp. 84-97). New York: Basic Books

Freud, S. (1924). "The Passing of the Oedipus Complex". In E. Jones (Ed.), J. Riviere (trans.), *Sigmund Freud, Collected Papers, Volume II* (1959, pp. 269-276). New York: Basic Books

Freud, S. (1940). *An Outline of Psychoanalysis. Standard Edition*, 23: 144–207.

Freud, S. (1960). *The Ego and the Id.* (Joan Riviere, trans.). New York: W.W. Norton and Company.

Freud, S. (1961). *Beyond the Pleasure Principle.* (James Strachey, trans.). New York: W.W. Norton & Company.

Freud, S. (1962). *Three Essays on the Theory of Sexuality* (James Strachey, trans.). New York: Basic Books

Grasse, P.P. (1977). *Evolution of Living Organisms*. New York: Academic

Grof, S. (1996). *Realms of the Human Unconscious: Observations from LSD Research.* London: Souvenir Press

Guattari, F. (1989/2013). *Schizoanalytic Cartographies* (Andrew Goffey, trans.). London & New York: Bloomsbury

Harlow, H. F. & Zimmermann, R. R. (1959) "Affectional Responses in the Infant Monkey". *Science*, Vol 130, Aug, 421-432

Hebb, D.O. (1949/2002). *The Organization of Behaviour: A Neuropsychological Theory*. New York: Wiley

Hellingwerf, K.J. (2005). "Bacterial observations: a rudimentary form of intelligence?". *Trends Microbiol*, 13:152–158

Hellingwerf, K.J., Postma, P.W., Tommassen, J., Westerhoff, H.V. (1995). "Signal transduction in bacteria: phosphoneural network in *Escherichia coli*". *FEMS Microbiol Rev*, 16: 309–321

Hoffer, S.M., Westerhoff, H.V., Hellingwerf, K.J., Postma, P.W., Tommassen, J. (2001). "Autoamplification of a two component regulatory system results in learning behaviour". *J Bacteriol*, 183:4914–4917

Hoffman, A. (1979/1983). *LSD: My Problem Child: Reflections on Sacred Drugs, Mysticism, and Science* (Jonathan Ott, trans.). Sarasota: Multidisciplinary Association for Psychedelic Studies (MAPS)

Huxley, A. (1954/2009). *The Doors of Perception*. New York: Harper Perennial Modern Classics

Janiger, O. & Rios, M.D. (2003). *LSD, Spirituality, and the Creative Process*. Rochester: Park Street Press

Kasem, A. (2017). *Whose Unconscious Is It?*. CreateSpace

Kasem, A. (2018). *The Science of Self-Actualization*. CreateSpace

Klossowski, P. (1997). *Nietzsche and the Vicious Circle*. (Daniel W. Smith, trans.). London: Athlone Press

La Cerra, P. (2003). "The first law of psychology is the second law of thermodynamics: the energetic model of the mind and the generation of human psychological phenomena". *Hum Nature Rev*, 3:440–447

La Cerra, P. & Bingham, R. (1998). "The adaptive nature of the human neuro-cognitive architecture: an alternative model". *Proc Natl Acad Sci USA*, 95: 11290–11294

La Rochefoucauld. (2007). *Collected Maxims and Other Reflections* (E.H. Blackmore, A.M. Blackmore, & F. Giguère, trans.). Oxford: Oxford University Press

Lawrence, D.H. (1976). *Aaron's Rod*. New York: Penguin

Leopardi, G. (2017). *Moral Fables* (J.G. Nichols, trans.). London: Alma Classics

Marcuse, H. (1955/1966). *Eros and Civilization: A Philosophical Inquiry into Freud*. Boston: Beacon Press

Nakagaki, T., Yamada, H., Toth, A. (2000). "Maze solving by an amoeboid organism". *Nature*, 407:470

Nasio, J.D. (2005/2010). *Oedipus: The Most Crucial Concept in Psychoanalysis*. Albany: SUNY Press

Nietzsche, F. (2000). *Basic Writings of Nietzsche*. (Walter Kaufmann, trans.). New York: The Modern Library

Nietzsche, F. (1982). *The Portable Nietzsche*. (Walter Kaufmann, trans.). New York: Penguin Books

Nietzsche, F. (2003). *Writings from the Late Notebooks*. (Kate Sturge, trans.). Cambridge: Cambridge University Press

Panksepp, J. (1998). *Affective Neuroscience: The Foundations of Human and Animal Emotions*. New York: Oxford University Press.

Proust, M. (1981/1993). *In Search of Lost Time, Volume IV: Sodom and Gomorrah* (C.K. Scott Moncrieff, trans.). New York: Modern Library

Reich, W. (1980). *The Mass Psychology of Fascism* (3rd ed.). New York: Farrar, Straus and Giroux.

Savic, I. & Lindstrom, P. (2008). "PET and MRI show differences in cerebral asymmetry and functional connectivity between homo- and heterosexual subjects". *PNAS*, 27: 9403-9408

Schenberg, E.E. (2018). "Psychedelic-Assisted Psychotherapy: A Paradigm Shift in Psychiatric Research and Development". *Frontiers in Pharmacology*, 9: 733.

Solms, M., & Turnbull, O. (2002). *The Brain and the Inner World: An Introduction to the Neuroscience of Subjective Experience*. London: Karnac Books.

Stanislavski, C. (1936/1964). *An Actor Prepares* (Elizabeth Reynolds Hapgood, trans.). New York: Routledge

Stendhal. (1957). *Love*. (Gilbert and Suzanne Sale, trans.). New York, NY: Penguin Books

Stenhouse, D. (1974). *The Evolution of Intelligence – A General Theory and Some of its Implications*. London: Allen and Unwin

Torok, M. (1994). "The Meaning of Penis Envy in Women." In M. Torok & N. Abraham (Eds.), *The Shell and the Kernel: Renewals of Psychoanalysis, Volume 1* (pp. 41-73). Chicago and London: The University of Chicago Press

Trewavas. (2006). "The Green Plant as an Intelligent Organism." In F. Baluška, S. Mancuso, D. Volkmann (Eds.), *Communication in Plants: Neuronal Aspects of Plant Life* (pp. 1-18). Berlin & Heidelberg: Springer-Verlag

Tupper, K.W., Wood, E., Yensen, R., Johnson, M.W. (2015). "Psychedelic medicine: a re-emerging therapeutic paradigm". *CMAJ, 187* (14): 1054–9.

Warwick, K. (2001). *The Quest for Intelligence*. London: Piatkus

Wilson, T.D., Lindsey, S., Schooler, T.Y.. (2000). "A Model of Dual Attitudes". *Psychological Review (107)*, 1: 101-126

Note: We have used abbreviations to designate the following works by Nietzsche in the main body of our text:
BGE = Beyond Good and Evil
GM = On the Genealogy of Morals
TI = The Twilight of the Idols
WLN = Writings from the Late Notebooks, trans. Kate Sturge

We have followed convention in citing Nietzsche's texts using the numbers of his aphorisms; the numbers in our citations of Nietzsche refer to the numbers of aphorisms, and not to page numbers. We have worked mostly from Walter Kaufmann's translations, collected in *Basic Writings of Nietzsche* and *The Portable Nietzsche*.

www.ingramcontent.com/pod-product-compliance
Lightning Source LLC
Chambersburg PA
CBHW031253250726
48655CB00005B/2201